Ben-Gurion and the Palestinian Arabs

BEN-GURION
and the Palestinian Arabs
From Peace to War

SHABTAI TEVETH

Oxford New York
OXFORD UNIVERSITY PRESS
1985

Oxford University Press

Oxford London New York Toronto
Delhi Bombay Calcutta Madras Karachi
Kuala Lumpur Singapore Hong Kong Tokyo
Nairobi Dar es Salaam Cape Town
Melbourne Auckland

and associated companies in
Beirut Berlin Ibadan Mexico City Nicosia

Published by Oxford University Press, Inc.,
200 Madison Avenue,
New York, New York 10016

Library of Congress Cataloging in Publication Data
Teveth, Shabtai, 1925–
Ben-Gurion and the Palestinian Arabs.
Bibliography: p. Includes index.
1. Ben-Gurion, David, 1886–1973—Views on Jewish-Arab relations.
2. Jewish-Arab relations—1917– . I. Title.
Ds125.3.B37T47 1985 956.94'05'0924 84–29618
ISBN 0–19–503562–3

Printing (last digit): 9 8 7 6 5 4 3 2 1
Printed in the United States of America

The clear, aware, and courageous perception of the recesses and fathomless depths of reality; and the alert and intuitive harkening to the forces of change and motives of the future which are the heartbeats of ever-renewing history—on these, the Zionist policy of the workers' movement rests.

David Ben-Gurion, in his introduction to *We and Our Neighbors*, May 1931

Preface

There are a number of sound reasons for examining David Ben-Gurion's thinking on the Palestinian Arabs. As a Zionist theoretician and statesman, Ben-Gurion grappled with the question of relations between Arabs and Jews for over sixty-five years, from his arrival in Ottoman Palestine in 1906, until his death in 1973. More than any other Zionist leader, he had the opportunity to implement his ideas as a maker of policy. In the forty-two years between 1921 and 1963—during which he served as labor leader, Zionist statesman, and the Prime Minister of an independent Israel—his influence grew to have a decisive effect on Zionist policy; Israel came to view the Arabs, to a great extent, through the eyes of David Ben-Gurion.

Zionists called the complex issues surrounding relations between Arabs and Jews in Palestine "the Arab question." Ben-Gurion noted that this was "an imprecise definition." He recognized that this "tragic question of fate" arose only as a consequence of Zionism, and so was a "question of Zionist fulfillment in the light of Arab reality."[1] In other words, this was a Zionist rather than an Arab question, posed to Zionists who were perplexed about how they could fulfill their aspirations in a land inhabited by an Arab majority.

More than any Zionist leader, Ben-Gurion dwelt on this question, in a perpetual search for a satisfactory answer. From the outset, he was one of the few leaders of Labor Zionism who sought to anchor the Jewish right to Palestine in something other than historical argument and nationalist myth. The claims of Zionism derived from its character as a movement of peace, justice, and progress. And so in his thought, one can trace an evolution, away from a vision of Zionism as a movement for absolute justice bearing a universal message, a movement of peace and constructive labor. His revised view of Zionism, forged by events and the specter of the Holocaust, was of a movement for relative justice with the Jews its sole concern, a movement prepared to wage war and to take the country, by force, if necessary.

Ben-Gurion's thought, then, was influential and exemplary. On these accounts alone, it warrants study. Yet it has also been misinterpreted. There is a view abroad that Ben-Gurion, in many important respects, was naive about the depth of Arab political aspirations and Arab determination to resist the Zionist transformation of Palestine. This view rests almost exclusively on Ben-Gurion's public pronouncements, taking these to be a full expression of his conviction. A comparison of these pronouncements with Ben-Gurion's private reflections, committed to paper in his diary, in letters, and in the protocols of closed meetings, however, reveals a far more complex picture. For Ben-Gurion was a political man and was quite capable of pragmatic insincerity. To bring the maximum number of Jews to Palestine's shores, he was prepared to "sup with the devil,"[2] so he hardly would have shunned a tactic of dissimulation for moral reasons. Which of Ben-Gurion's stated views arose from genuine conviction, and which from pragmatic calculation? The question is difficult to answer, particularly since Ben-Gurion, like other Labor Zionists, had every reason to deny the claim of Palestine's Arabs for recognition as a political community. To have offered such recognition in public would have cast doubt on Zionism as a movement that aspired to absolute justice for Jew and Arab alike.

Not only is it important to separate Ben-Gurion's convictions from his tactics; it is essential to appreciate the transformations those tactics underwent during many years of shifting political sands in Palestine. In the years between 1910 and 1918, Ben-Gurion declared to all who would listen that a fundamental conflict divided Jews and Arabs over Palestine; from 1918 to 1929, he denied that any such conflict existed and argued that such misunderstanding as existed between Jews and Arabs would be dispelled by the coming social revolution. From 1929 until 1936, Ben-Gurion again recognized in public that Jews and Arabs were at cross-purposes, but held that differences could be resolved through negotiations between Arab nationalists and Zionist leaders; from 1936, he admitted that Jewish and Arab differences were fundamental, and no longer did he believe that they could be resolved peaceably. This evolution reflected a constant reassessment of tactics. But Ben-Gurion took all of these positions to achieve, in different circumstances, two unchanging goals: to bring about the immigration of endangered Jews on such scale as to render them a majority in Palestine and to win the support of a world power, preferably the one that ruled Palestine, for the fledgling Zionist enterprise.

I wish to offer my special thanks to Professor Elie Kedourie, who convinced me that Ben-Gurion's thinking on the Arabs deserved separate study, although the initial inspiration emerged from the larger Hebrew biography that I have prepared and begun to publish. In the course of collecting archival material, I incurred a number of debts to helpful institutions and persons. I wish to offer my thanks to the Central Zionist Archives, under the direction of Dr. Michael Heymann, and to Mr. Israel Philip, for their kind assistance; to the Institute for the Legacy of David Ben-Gurion and its director, Dr. Meir

Avizohar, an old and faithful friend who assisted me with sources and advice; and to Haim Israeli, former secretary to David Ben-Gurion, who filled some of my documentary gaps and turned my attention to points I had overlooked. I am most grateful to the Nahman Karni Memorial Fund for its support.

My thanks also go to Professor Itamar Rabinovich, head of the Dayan Center for Middle Eastern and African Studies at Tel Aviv University, for his sound advice. I owe special thanks to Professor Yoram Dinstein, rector of Tel Aviv University, who read the manuscript with great diligence and offered useful comments; and to Professor Yehoshua Porath of the Hebrew University in Jerusalem, who answered all of my questions with patience and generosity. I should also like to offer special thanks to my secretary, Mrs. Rachel Rader, who withstood the hardships of researching Ben-Gurion's life with me. Finally, it gives me particular pleasure to thank Mr. Gershom Schocken, my long-time editor and publisher, for his unstinting guidance and support. It was he who led me to undertake my study of Ben-Gurion's life.

This work is a rendition in English of a rather weightier tome in Hebrew. The English version is distinguished from the Hebrew by an economy of expression and documentation, which I believe will be appreciated by the English reader. My deepest thanks to Dr. Martin Kramer, of the Dayan Center for Middle Eastern and African Studies, at Tel Aviv University, for making it possible.

Tel Aviv S.T.
September 1984

Contents

Ben-Gurion and the Palestinian Arabs

GLOSSARY

Poalei Zion "Workers of Zion," Zionist Marxist parties, in Europe, America, and Palestine.

Ahdut Ha'avodah United Labor, a socialist Zionist party, formed in February 1919, by the union of Palestine Poalei Zion with other labor bodies.

Mapai United Labor Party of Palestine, formed in January 1930, by the union of Ahdut Ha'avodah with Hapoel Hatzair and other bodies, for many years the ruling party in the Zionist organization and in the Jewish community in Palestine, and later in Israel.

Histadrut General Jewish Workes Federation of Palestine, founded December 1920, the dominant body in the Yishuv.

Yishuv Community, the Jewish Community of Palestine, mostly Zionist, a term used from the end of the previous century until the formation of the State of Israel.

Old Yishuv The religious Jewish community of Palestine, prior to establishment of the Yishuv, the anti-Zionist part of which opposed the Yishuv.

Avodah Ivrit Hebrew Labor, a principle conceived by Hapoel Hatzair and Ahdut Ha'avodah, and later made into a Histadrut rule that Jews in Palestine be employed by Jews and Arabs by Arabs.

Haganah Defense, the Zionist defense underground in Palestine, on which the Israeli Army was later founded.

Arab Executive Committee Representative body of Arab political parties in Palestine.

Arab Higher Committee Superseded the Arab Executive Committee.

Jewish Agency Agency recognized under the Mandate to represent Jewish and Zionist interests in Palestine.

Zionist Executive A coalition elected in the Zionist biannual world congresses to head the Jewish Agency.

Havlagah Restraint, Zionist policy of nonretaliation during the Arab Rebellion and the Riots of 1936–1939.

1
First Encounters

David Ben-Gurion, born in Plonsk, Poland, in 1886, described himself as a Zionist from birth. At the age of three, he learned Hebrew on his grandfather's lap and began to read the Old Testament before he attended the traditional *heder*. It was then that he first heard from his father about *Eretz Israel*—the Land of Israel, Palestine. Father showed son the representations of Palestine's fruits on the ark in their synagogue. But Ben-Gurion was unsatisfied, insisting that "these are only pictures. I want the real Palestine."[1]

His public career began after the First Zionist Congress in 1897, when he persuaded his schoolmates to contribute one *kopeck* a week from their pocket money to purchase one *shekel* issued by the Zionist Organization. In December 1900, at the age of fourteen, he and two of his friends founded a youth club known as *Ezra*, with the twofold aim of encouraging Hebrew studies and promoting emigration to the holy land. After the Kishinev pogroms of 1903, the *Ezra* youths fanned out to collect contributions for the victimized families. The misery of Russian Jewry, though never the foundation stone of his Zionism, did urge Ben-Gurion toward love of Zion, and sharpened a yearning for the land of his forefathers, handed down to him generation by generation. The appearance of Herzl stirred in young Ben-Gurion and his friends a messianic longing for the sovereign renewal of Israel in her homeland. It was not religious belief that moved him. He shed religion following his bar mitzvah, perhaps even earlier. His messianism stemmed rather from his conviction that the redemption of Israel was very close at hand, around history's bend. All that was needed was energetic action by Zionists, and he himself would live to see that long-awaited redemption.

In 1904, Ben-Gurion addressed *Ezra* on the mission of the Jewish people to spread the message of Moses and the Prophets throughout the world; he was as yet uncommitted to socialist doctrine. Only in the fall of 1905, in a climate of agitation against plans for the legislative Duma, did Ben-Gurion join the Social-Democratic Jewish Workers' Party—Poalei Zion—and thus identify himself as a Marxist. And so he became a Labor Zionist only a year before his arrival in Palestine. Ben-Gurion played no role of any note in the ideological and theoretical debate within the Polish Poalei Zion. Nor had he any contact with the party's founding fathers in Russia. But there is no doubt that he read the articles of the theoretician of socialist Zionism, Ber Borochov, while still in Poland. Ben-Gurion was present at an ideological colloquium held by Poalei Zion in Warsaw, to discuss the prognosis set forth by Borochov in his article, "On the Question of Zion and Territory." Borochov had sought to prove that Palestine, because of inevitable economic and political developments, would be the only country able to meet the practical needs of the Jewish liberation movement. From his own disappointment in the Diaspora and the limited possibilities for Jews to flourish within it, Borochov reached the conclusion that worsening conditions would drive the Jews in their masses toward Palestine. But although he drew on Borochov's idiom and intellectual assumptions, the Marxist veneer applied to Ben-

Gurion during that year in the Polish Poalei Zion proved thin and transitory. Once the fashion had passed, Ben-Gurion would declare that "I am not a Marxist."[2] In the reflections of old age, he finally determined that "I believe that the inspiration of the Bible sustained us, returned us to the land, and created the state . . . all of my humanitarian and Jewish values, I drew from the Bible."[3]

The Arabs of Palestine were of no concern to Ben-Gurion, but in this respect he was typical of the Zionists of the time. Yet, although he never gave the issue any thought, he did pick up a few ideas that later affected his approach to the question of Jewish-Arab relations. Ben-Gurion was well acquainted with the doctrines of the Jewish socialist and anti-Zionist Bund, and while he naturally opposed them, he nonetheless found some Bundist arguments compelling. On this account, he would rarely speak of the historical rights of the Jewish people to Palestine, but preferred to emphasize the Jewish right to work the land, to settle in uninhabited reaches and make them blossom. He held the right to work as the highest of values. It was Ben-Gurion's position that the Jewish right to determine the future of the country was distinct and superior to any right stemming from history, Jewish or other. The land belonged to those prepared to work it and develop it, and it was immoral to deny a dynamic people the opportunity to better the country through its own labors. "We have the right to build and be built in Palestine"; "we will win the country by building it"; "Palestine will be ours when we provide most of its builders and defenders." These were the credos he etched in Zionist doctrine.

As for the rights of the Arabs—the inhabitants of the country for many generations—he repeated word for word the doctrine of the Bund concerning the Jews of Russia and Poland. Just as the Jews had the right to see these countries as their own, so the Arabs enjoyed the same right in Palestine. "The Arab community in Palestine is an organic, inseparable part of the landscape. It is embedded in the country. The Arabs work the land, and will remain." Ben-Gurion even held that the Arabs had full rights in Palestine, "since the only right by which a people can claim to possess a land indefinitely is the right conferred by willingness to work."[4] They had the same opportunity to establish that right as the Zionists did.

But these seeds of ideas were to germinate in Ben-Gurion's political thought only later, in 1913, 1915, 1930, and in some instances as late as 1948. Ben-Gurion was certainly unburdened by such concerns when he set sail on a Russian ship bound for Palestine in August 1906. Only twenty years of age, his eyes were dazzled by the shining land of his dreams, which no Arab could eclipse.

It was on a ship bound for Palestine, among the passengers, that Ben-Gurion saw Arabs for the first time. Along with his fellow travelers from Plonsk, he regarded them with anxious curiosity, and over a shared pot of coffee tried to converse with them. The result delighted him. "They made a very good impression upon us," Ben-Gurion wrote to his father.[5] "They are nearly all good-hearted, and are easily befriended. One might say that they are like big children. We met a few, and they clung to us for the whole journey. They sang for us, entertained us, and tried to amuse us as much as possible." He felt a special companionship with an Arab from Beirut, a military doctor with the rank of captain, "who befriended us like a brother." When seasickness struck Ben-Gurion and his colleagues, the doctor applied compresses to their heads, and gave them sweets. "He began to learn Hebrew from us, and stammered Hebrew words throughout the journey. When we said goodbye, he gave us his address, and urged us to visit him when we came to Beirut." This, then, was the Arab reception for a Jew from Plonsk making his way to Zion.

On the morning of September 7, 1906, the ship dropped anchor off the port of Jaffa, and Ben-Gurion grew apprehensive: "The harbor suddenly was filled with skiffs, and Arabs clambered up the sides of our ship. The shouting and shoving were awful." The chaos lasted but a moment. As was the custom of the place, Arab porters lifted up passengers and baggage alike in their burly arms, and carried them off the ship into the skiffs. At shore they again carried their passengers and deposited them on dry ground. On this intimate contact, and on the very fact that he was borne to the land of Israel in Arab arms, Ben-Gurion said nothing.[6]

For from the moment he touched shore, Ben-Gurion thought only of the land of his dreams and its new inhabitants, the Jews. He had no thoughts to spare for Jaffa and its Arab residents. The bustling Oriental city, with its minarets and churches, a city the likes of which he had never seen before, did not enchant or engross him. "Jaffa is not pretty," he wrote to his father. "As in any Oriental city, the streets are narrow and winding. An awful dust hangs over the marketplace, for there are no pavement stones." Some merit was to be found in "a hill planted with cedars and palms. These are the country's most beautiful trees." But he praised only the natural flora and showed no interest in the city's inhabitants or their handiwork. Ben-Gurion spent exactly seven hours in Jaffa; he wrote to his father that he had no desire to stay longer, "because of the dust." In later years he wrote that "I saw an uglier exile in Jaffa than in Plonsk. It was true that there was a street which bore a Hebrew name, Neveh Shalom, but it was full of Arab shopkeepers who sat about smoking their nargilahs. Among them were a few Jews. It made a bad impression upon me."[7]

He had eyes only for the new and renewed Palestine. When he heard Hebrew spoken in the streets and saw it inscribed on shop signs, his heart opened up: "I felt waves of joy sweep through me from within," he wrote to his father. In every Hebrew thing, he saw the "buds of renaissance!" A Hebrew lad "galloping confidently on a spirited horse," or a "Hebrew girl of eight years riding upon a laden donkey"—"These are visions of the rebirth!" Ben-Gurion made up his mind to head directly for Petah-Tikvah, the "Metropole," as he called it, of the "Hebrew republics"—the Jewish agricultural settlements.

Here was a portent of things to come. The Arabs, whether affable "big children" or the inhabitants of winding, dust-filled alleyways, did not concern him. He counted the hours he spent in Jaffa. In his indifference, Ben-Gurion was not exceptional. Many of his contemporaries in this wave of Jewish immigration, the Second *Aliya*, were completely uninterested in the Arabs. And in fact, the Arab national awakening was yet young and did not command or deserve the newcomers' attention. Only on account of his later role does Ben-Gurion's attitude warrant particular examination, for the distinction that he drew so early between Arab and Jew would later have many and varied repercussions.

On the afternoon of that first day, Ben-Gurion set out for Petah-Tikvah by foot, and arrived in late evening. It was here that he first viewed the Arab laborer at work, and in less than a month he had formulated an approach that drew a distinction between Arab and Jewish worker. The citrus groves of Petah-Tikvah filled thousands of acres and required many working hands, particularly at harvest time. The farmers preferred to employ cheap Arab labor, and in order to find work, Ben-Gurion and other Jewish fieldhands had to compete with Arabs who were prepared to do the job for less. In this competition, many of the Jewish workers of the Second *Aliya* fared poorly. Ben-Gurion had no doubt that if the Jewish farmers of Petah-Tikvah and other settlements would only favor Jewish workers, still more opportunities for Jewish employment and immigration would arise. But at this stage, Ben-Gurion was still far from the slogan of *Avodah Ivrit*—the demand that Jews employ only Jews—and admitted the need of Jews to employ Arabs in a period of rapid growth. He simply called for an increase in the number of Jewish workers in certain branches of the economy, arguing that this would also benefit the Arabs. In 1915 he expressed his concept in this formula: "Our renewal in this land will come through renewal of the land itself, and that means the renewal of its Arab inhabitants." As late as the 1930s, he returned to the early example of Petah-Tikvah in support of this claim. On land from which twenty impoverished Arab families had scratched out a livelihood, the Jews of Petah-Tikvah had established a settlement able to maintain two thousand families, both Jewish and Arab, in comfort.[8]

But on the issue of worker unionization, Ben-Gurion immediately insisted on segregation along national lines. A month after his arrival, he returned to Jaffa for the constituent meeting of a new party, Poalei Zion. There, the newcomer met with dizzying success; he was elected to the central committee of the party and to the chairmanship of the party's platform committee. In filling these tasks, he clashed ideologically with a leftist faction that favored a strictly Marxist platform, emphasized class struggle, and proposed that the workers' union to be created by the party be open to Arab and Jew alike. Ben-Gurion headed the opposing, nationalist faction, and demanded that the union be open to Jews only. It was Ben-Gurion who ultimately prevailed.[9]

Four days after the constituent meeting, on October 8, 1906, the ten members of the platform committee met in an Arab hostel in Ramleh. For three days they sat on stools debating, and at night they slept on mats. An Arab boy brought them coffee in small cups. They left the hostel only to grab an occasional bite in the marketplace. On the first evening, they stole three hours to tour the marketplace of Ramleh and the ruins of the nearby fortress. Ben-Gurion remarked only on the buildings, ruins, and scenery. He gave no thought to the Arabs, their problems, their social conditions, or their cultural life. Nor had he yet acquainted himself with the Jewish community of Palestine. In all of Palestine there were

700,000 inhabitants, only 55,000 of whom were Jews, and only 550 of these were pioneers. But this reality did not distract the drafters of the platform, who could just as well have written it while still in Russia. Certainly in Ben-Gurion's case, the platform had taken form in his mind before he knew anything of his new country and its inhabitants.

Once again two factions clashed, the leftist and the nationalist. The former wanted a purely Marxist program, while the latter, in Ben-Gurion's words, "worked to insert a nationalist element, the Jewish problem in its entirety, and, above all, the Zionist demands concerning Palestine." The leftists sought to deny the national conflict that might stem from Jewish immigration by positing the creation of a single Arab-Jewish proletariat struggling for the establishment of a socialist state. Ben-Gurion and the nationalists held that the Jewish proletariat would emerge from a developed capitalist economy—a Jewish economy—while an Arab proletariat would emerge separately from a feudal, underdeveloped economy in which "the intensity of labor does not play an important role"—that is, an Arab economy. This was the first mention of a division of the economy of Palestine along national lines.[10]

In a conference held on January 5, 1907, the platform and program drafted in Ramleh were approved.[11] These included two major points inserted by Ben-Gurion and his followers: the mention of "national struggle" alongside "class struggle," and the observation that "the developing capitalism of Palestine requires educated and energetic workers," meaning Jews. The conference also adopted maximum and minimum objectives, as then was customary among socialist parties. The maximum program called for the establishment of a socialist society through class struggle. The minimum aims were the establishment of an independent Jewish state in Palestine, with the possibility of interim autonomy for the Jewish population of the country. This minimum program also provided for the establishment of Jewish trade unions, which Ben-Gurion set about organizing. The division and segregation between Jewish and Arab workers became principles applied in practice, permanent fixtures in the constellation of Labor Zionist thought and practice.

Ben-Gurion did not remain for long on the central committee of Poalei Zion. In the fall of 1907 he left for the Galilee. But before his move, he had the opportunity to meet Herzl's successor as president of the Zionist Organization, David Wolffsohn, at a reception in Wolffsohn's honor. On that occasion, Ben-Gurion spoke on behalf of Poalei Zion, emphasizing immigration and settlement.[12] He also urged that settlements on Jewish National Fund land employ only Jewish workers, not Arabs. It was necessary "once and for all" to enforce the principle of *Avodah Ivrit*. Ben-Gurion was still far from demanding exclusively Jewish employment throughout the Jewish sector, public and private. But he had taken an initial step in that direction, by insisting on the exclusive employment of Jewish agricultural labor on national land.

The concept of *Avodah Ivrit* taking form in Ben-Gurion's mind became still clearer during the party's conference held on September 23, 1907, after his move to the Galilee.[13] At this point, the party and its central committee were in the hands of Itzhak Ben-Zvi, who had arrived in Jaffa in March as an emissary of Poalei Zion in Russia. Under Ben-Zvi's leadership, the party leaned leftwards. But Ben-Gurion's remarks to the conference reflected his own disillusionment with Borochov's doctrines and his dissatisfaction with the Russian influence prevalent in the party. "The members from Russia have brought with them Russian rhetoric, concepts, and principles," he complained, "and so have created a Russian party here." "Let us finally free ourselves from the Russian legacy." He meant that the nationalist and Zionist role of the party had to be clarified and stressed.

In his speech, Ben-Gurion argued that the principal task of the Jewish proletariat was to build an independent Jewish state. Class struggle in Palestine thus differed from class struggle in any other country. As socialists everywhere, the members of Poalei Zion had a duty to organize workers and guide them in that battle. But there was still another task—to promote Jewish immigration and build the state. And so any labor union that was to organize Jewish laborers could not rest content with improving working conditions. It first had a national mission to fulfill. This was an unequivocal argument for the primacy of national over class interests.

From this vision of a national mission arose Ben-Gurion's opposition to Arab membership in the party and the trade unions it was to establish. Could the Arab worker truly be a partner in the national task of the Jewish worker? Could he really wish to encourage and increase Jewish immigration? Could he be expected to aid the establishment of an independent Jewish state? Reflections on these questions led to the organizational division of Jewish and Arab labor that young Ben-Gurion championed.

In the fall of 1907, Ben-Gurion left Jaffa, Petah-Tikvah, and party politics for the Galilee. He spent most of the next three years pioneering in Galilean settlements and in Zichron Yaakov. His encounters with Arabs during this period differed from those he had known hitherto. The question of Arab *versus* Jewish labor was not an issue in the Galilee, and only in the settlement of Menahemiyya did the farmers employ mostly Arabs, as in Petah-Tikvah. Because Ben-Gurion wished to prove "that we are better workers," he took employment in Menahemiyya with a farmer who had two other fieldhands, a Jew and an Arab. The competition then began. The two Jews worked intentionally at breakneck speed; the Arab, who could not keep up with them, "pleaded with us that we not put him to shame, and not hurry so much in our work."[14] Perhaps this inspired Ben-Gurion's later claim that the Jewish laborer, despite the fact that he asked a higher

wage, gave his employer a better return, as he was "more intelligent and diligent" than the Arab.[15]

But in the Galilee, Ben-Gurion's encounters with Arabs were marred for the first time by violence. He did not witness the first bloody clash between Jews and Arabs after his arrival, the February 1908 "Purim Incident" in Jaffa. On the eve of the holiday, Jewish and Arab workers fought a nasty brawl that ended in the death of one Arab. Soldiers then stormed a Jewish hostel to seize the Jews involved, and opened fire, wounding fourteen persons. Ben-Gurion, at that time in the Galilean collective of Sejera, recounted the incident in a letter to his father.[16] He described the initial disturbance as a commonplace occurrence, "because the city Arabs, mostly Egyptian, hate us." Arabs who were not Egyptians did not. And given Arab temperament, the incident was not exceptional: "Such events have happened often, at various times and places, and not just between Jews and Arabs, but more commonly among the Arabs themselves, between one tribe and another, or one village and another." In other words, assaults on Jews did not stem from some rooted national animosity.

Then an event occurred that deeply influenced Ben-Gurion's attitude toward the Arab issue. While in Sejera, a few of the collective's members secretly aspired to the creation of a Jewish army. As an initial step toward this distant goal, they sought work as watchmen. This profession in Jewish settlements had been the traditional preserve of Arabs and particularly Circassians, but at Sejera, Jewish watchmen succeeded in displacing them. Ben-Gurion also took a loan from the group and bought his own personal sidearm, a Browning pistol. He and the others then outlasted the attempts by Circassians to frighten them with gunfire in the night, and Ben-Gurion rejoiced that "the first stronghold has been conquered."[17]

At this stage, Ben-Gurion viewed the task of Jewish watchmen as simply defending life and property against the covetous designs of neighbors and the pilfering habits of vandals and robbers. That there might be a broader security aspect—self-defense to deter hostile acts directed specifically against Jewish settlement in Palestine—did not occur to him. Ben-Gurion did not yet define the Arabs as a political entity capable of aiding or defeating Zionist aims. In Sejera he did hire a teacher to instruct him in Arabic, and he began to study the language. But he did this not to acquaint himself with the ways of the Arabs, but because he had decided to learn law and thought that, as a lawyer in Palestine, he might need Arab clients to make ends meet. In any case, he soon abandoned his studies. But then came the incident that opened his eyes and led him to recognize the emergence of an Arab sentiment hostile to the Zionist vision.

The purchase of land in the Galilee for Jewish settlement stirred opposition among Arab peasants forced off land sold by their landlords. Disputes over property intensified following the Ottoman constitutional revolution of 1908 and the consequent *hurriyya*—"liberty" that soon degenerated into licentiousness. Relations between Sejera and the nearby Arab village of Kafr Kanna also deteriorated, and Arabs began to trespass on the Jewish settlement's lands. The tension grew throughout the spring of 1909 and broke into violence in April. A Jewish photographer on the way from Haifa to Sejera was beaten and robbed by Arabs from Kafr Kanna, but the victim managed to inflict a mortal gunshot wound on one of his assailants. The peasants of Kafr Kanna retaliated by stealing cattle from Sejera and sending their herds into the settlement's fields. There was even some deliberate destruction of Sejera's crops. The situation grew worse, and Ben-Gurion kept his Browning pistol at the ready.

And then on a rainy Monday, April 12, 1909, two Arabs shot and killed Sejera's watchman, Israel Korngold. This was simply bait for a carefully laid trap. For when Sejera's alarm bell rang, and the settlers—Ben-Gurion among them—gave chase to the Arabs, they stumbled into additional ambushes. The search for the assailants continued in driving rain until nightfall. When two of Sejera's settlers came into view, in hot pursuit of three fleeing Arabs, Ben-Gurion and two Jewish farmers, one of them a certain Shimon Melamed, hurried to cut off their escape. But the Arabs led them almost directly into an ambush, and Ben-Gurion and his fellows turned on their heels. "Then all the inhabitants of the [Arab] village lit after us," wrote Ben-Gurion. The retreat was sounded from Sejera. Suddenly Ben-Gurion heard Melamed's voice: "They've shot me!" An Arab hiding in the brush had shot Melamed through the heart. He fell, and by the time Ben-Gurion arrived at his side, he was already dead. The tragic event was inscribed in Zionist annals as the most trying test of fire Jewish settlers had endured till that time.[18]

After the shootings, there was much talk in Galilean settlements about new measures for self-defense. But negotiations for a *sulha*—a reconcilation—soon began with the neighboring Arab villages. The public ways still were not safe. In August 1909, Ben-Gurion tied on his satchel and walked alone from Sejera toward the nearby Jewish settlement of Yavniel. On the way, he was accosted by an Arab robber brandishing a dagger. Because of their proximity to an Arab village, Ben-Gurion did not shoot him with his pistol. But the robber attempted to wrest the gun away, and the two wrestled in the dirt. The Arab finally grabbed Ben-Gurion's satchel and ran off, but not before wounding Ben-Gurion with the dagger. Ben-Gurion was proud that he had kept his wits about him and had not shot his assailant, thus reopening the circle of recrimination in the Galilee.[19]

Not until thirty years later did Ben-Gurion reveal his innermost thoughts about the bloody encounters at Sejera. In a letter to his wife, he described an anxiety rarely equaled in his life.[20] It arose, he explained, not simply from fear of life-threatening danger, but from distress over a new situation, a turning point. In Sejera, he wrote, he saw for the first time "the severity and dangers of the 'Arab problem.'"[21] The political lesson that he had learned, he shared with his political party in a lecture delivered in Jaffa in October 1910, and with a wider public in an article in the party newspaper *Ha'ahdut.*[22] By that time, he had moved to Jerusalem to work as an editor of the paper.

He was no longer blind to the Arabs but now recognized a conflict of interests between them and the Jews. Ben-Gurion reached this conclusion by analyzing the aftermath of the Young Turk revolution and *hurriyya* of 1908. It was paradoxical that the very revolution that had opened new possibilities for Jews in the Ottoman Empire to attain national autonomy also stirred national awakenings among the other subject peoples of the empire. There soon would develop "a pitched struggle and intense rivalry between the various peoples. Each will attempt to fortify its position in agriculture and industry, in trade and labor; to expand its political influence; to increase its strength and so dislodge its rival." Ben-Gurion made it clear to his audience that the Arabs were rivals pitted in the struggle against the Jews.

In his lecture, he knew to cite Negib Azoury's *Le Réveil de la nation arabe dans l'Asie turque*, which had appeared in Paris in 1905. Azoury, a Syrian Catholic, had been an assistant to the Ottoman governor of Jerusalem, and in 1904 he founded a *Ligue de la patrie arabe* whose slogan was "Arabia for the Arabs." The book expressed total opposition to the aspirations of the Jews of Palestine: "Both of these movements (Jewish and Arab) are destined to fight each other continually until one of them triumphs." In his lecture, Ben-Gurion described *Le Réveil* as a book about "the Jewish peril in Palestine," an impediment to the "creation of a great Arab empire" advocated by Azoury. Ben-Gurion regarded the book itself as "the work of an individual appealing to the great powers." But after 1908, he said, the campaign against the Jews of the country was no longer the work of one man. "Today we see many newspapers in Palestine, Syria, and Egypt opposed to us, and the disciples of Azoury no longer appeal to foreign governments, but direct their propaganda toward the Arab people and the Turkish government."

Clearly he had read or heard about what was being written in the Arabic press, particularly in *al-Karmil* of Haifa, which was known for its unbridled hostility to the "Zionist enemy" and the Zionist design "to conquer Palestine." Because of this press, said Ben-Gurion, "the government lately has taken a bad view of Jewish settlement in Palestine." "But even more saddening is the hatred of our Arab neighbors for us." It was this hatred that had prompted a series of assaults against Jewish settlements in Judea and the Galilee. No longer did Ben-Gurion excuse Arab attacks as local custom, mere banditry, or blood vengeance. These were evidence of hatred. The events of Sejera had opened his eyes. "The Arabs of Palestine are a mortal danger," he wrote. "Every worker must learn to defend himself."[23]

Ben-Gurion wrote his first account of the Sejera incidents seven years later in New York. The account gained wide circulation in the second, expanded edition of *Yizkor*, a memorial book to the slain settlers, which appeared in New York in 1916. The book enjoyed great popularity among American Jews, and evenings devoted to commemoration of the fallen drew large audiences. Only in the pro-Bundist *Forwards* was the book made the subject of scathing criticism.

"Jewish settlement in Palestine is built upon the ruin of the Arabs," wrote Moshe Olgin in his review of *Yizkor*.[24] The courage of the Jewish settlers moved him, yet one question pursued him throughout his reading of the book: "Who are these Arabs?" "The Jewish settlers fell in battle with the Arabs. But who is this mysterious enemy? Is he a tyrant who has enslaved the country, like the czar of Russia? Is he a foreigner who rules the country, as the Englishman rules Ireland? Is he an individual who rules through his money, like Rockefeller in Colorado? Or are these Arabs simply a band of robbers and murderers?" Olgin's answer to these questions was negative: "No. The Arabs are not at all like that. They are the established inhabitants of Palestine, who lived there for hundreds of years before the arrival of the Zionist settlers." In short, the Arabs were waging a people's war against the Jews, a silent, determined, systematic war, a just war against those seeking to deprive them of their land. Those slain Jewish watchmen and pioneers commemorated in *Yizkor* fell in a war of conquest and oppression.

Olgin thus shared Ben-Gurion's view that the bloody attacks on the settlements were motivated by hatred of Jews. But Ben-Gurion lost his temper on reading Olgin's article: "In my opinion, this is a hooliganistic article, an appeal for a pogrom against the Jews of Palestine. This is the first time that a Jewish newspaper has written of the Jews that they are robbers pursuing a policy of oppression and extortion, while the Arab thieves and robbers are made to be revolutionaries waging a sacred war." Ben-Gurion's reply was so severe that the editor of his own party's newspaper in America would not publish it.[25] It is significant that by 1916, Ben-Gurion was no longer maintaining, at least in public, that hatred had moved the Arabs to attack Jewish settlements. It was as though he had returned to his analysis that preceded his Jaffa speech of October 1910, for in his reply to Olgin, Ben-Gurion spoke only of "Arab thieves and robbers." But was this really a reappraisal or merely a new tactic?

For in 1911, not only did Ben-Gurion recognize the existence of Arab hatred, but even spoke of "Arab hatred that is growing still more intense."[26] Late in 1914 he asked: "Who is there who hates us as they do?"[27] Ben-Gurion had an explanation:

> This hatred originates with the Arab workers in Jewish settlements. Like any worker, the Arab worker detests his taskmaster and exploiter. But because this class conflict overlaps a national difference between farmers and workers, this hatred takes a national form. Indeed, the national overwhelms the class aspect of the conflict in the minds of the Arab working masses, and inflames an intense hatred toward the Jews.

But the Jewish farmer was not the only cause. On the Arab side were "the Christian clergy and missionaries." These "incited the people to rise against the Jews, to take their land, pillage their property and threaten their very lives."[28]

This was a Marxist class interpretation, which found the owners of property and the clergy guilty of exploitation. In this way, Ben-Gurion sought to believe—and to convince others—that there need not be a conflict between the Zionists and the country's Arab inhabitants. His interpretation left a door open to a solution: socialism would eradicate Arab hatred by liberating the Arab worker from his servitude and the grip of the clergy. And the influence of the clergy was limited in any event, to the Christian Arab population, whereas the overwhelming majority of Palestine's Arabs were Muslims. In the meantime, Ben-Gurion did not propose a dialogue with the Arabs of Palestine, or even with local Ottoman authorities, on whom the Jews could no longer rely. He stressed that "because our survival and future depend upon us alone," the Yishuv had to place its case directly before the central government in Istanbul.[29] Self-reliance, socialism, and the sympathy of the power that ruled the country—these three forces would combine to fulfill Zionist hopes and squelch national conflict.

2

In Exile and War

In October 1911, Ben-Gurion left Palestine to learn law. First he studied Turkish in Salonica and then, in August 1912, began full-time study in the faculty of law in Istanbul. His legal education was cut short by the outbreak of war in August 1914, while he spent summer vacation in Jerusalem. During his Turkish period, Ben-Gurion had almost no personal contact with Arabs, but they were never far from his thoughts on possible futures for Palestine.

Ben-Gurion emerged during these years as a determined advocate of "Ottomanization" of the Empire's Jewish population. He developed the idea in the Poalei Zion newspaper *Ha'ahdut*, which he had helped to found. *Ha'ahdut*—unity—implied not only the unification of the divided Jewish community in the Empire, but echoed the program of the Young Turks, whose slogan was *ittihad*—union—of all Ottoman subjects, and their Ottomanization. The editors of *Ha'ahdut* adopted this slogan as well, and expressed "our unequivocal recognition that the strength of the Ottoman state, a state comprised of peoples who differ widely in language, culture, race, and history, rests only in internal solidarity." In this union, recognition would be accorded to the "full, internal rights" of Turks, Bulgars, Armenians, Greeks, Arabs, and of course the Jews of Palestine, who were entitled to autonomous standing.[1]

Yet here was the rub. Most of the Jews in Palestine were not Ottoman citizens but foreigners careful to keep their foreign nationality. They thus continued to enjoy the immunities and consular protection afforded them under the capitulations. More than 40,000 Jews in Palestine still held Russian citizenship and could not elect or be elected to legislative or administrative office at any level. The Arabs, on the other hand, were enfranchised Ottoman citizens. They not only served on local councils, but Arab delegates sat in the parliament (*mejlis*) in Istanbul, where they were the only representatives from Palestine. The Arabs mattered most to Ben-Gurion in this broader Ottoman context. In the struggle Ben-Gurion anticipated between peoples of the Empire, the Arabs also would demand autonomy. They would compete with the Jews for the same prize, and run against them in the same lane. To defeat them, the Jews would have to resort to political action at the seat of Ottoman government. One of Ben-Gurion's principles was that the Yishuv had to be Ottomanized and, once enfranchised with the vote, become a political force in its own right. The Jews then could send their own representatives to sit in local councils and the *mejlis* in Istanbul, and could rely on other Jews in the civil service.[2]

Ben-Gurion offered two arguments on behalf of Ottoman partiality toward the Jews in this contest. The first was the friendship and trust that Turkey, "both old and new," had in Jews. The Turks, claimed Ben-Gurion, knew that "of all peoples, only the Jews are the loyal friends of the Turkish people, because they have no designs for conquest as the others do." The second was the potential contribution of Jews to development. The new constitutional regime "needs financing and entrepreneurs who will launch industries and promote trade," and the Young Turks knew that "the Jews can fill the void and provide them with the human and material resources necessary for Turkey's development."[3] In the rivalry between Jews and Arabs, Turkey would have to take sides in accordance with its interests, and choose between today and tomorrow. Ben-Gurion based his arguments on the integration of the Jewish community as an expressly pro-Turkish element in the mix of Empire.

Throughout his law studies, Ben-Gurion sought to achieve for himself that which he advocated for the wider community. Jewish lawyers trained in Istanbul not only could introduce the Jews of Palestine to Ottoman ways, but eventually could be elected to legislative and administrative office. Ben-Gurion often would say that he went to Istanbul to study, in order that he might one day be elected to the *mejlis* as representative of the Yishuv. Sometimes he went so far as to say that he had hoped to become a minister in the Ottoman cabinet, "and there to defend Zionism."[4] Ben-Gurion even took on the appearance of an Ottoman gentleman of the bureaucratic class. He shed his loose Russian shirt for a dark, striped suit and coat over starched collar and tie; he grew a thick moustache to replace the shadow of one he had brought from Palestine. And above all, he donned a red fez.

The great difficulty with Ben-Gurion's plan was that the old Jewish community of Palestine, and the scattered Jewish population in the rest of the Empire, did not aspire to political autonomy. Nor were those Jews who held foreign citizenship prepared to exchange their protected status for the uncertainties of Ottoman nationality. In any event, Ben-Gurion's entire reading of Ottoman attitudes toward autonomy was based on his misunderstanding of the 1913 law for provincial reorganization. It was his belief that this reform had come to bestow greater freedom of action on provincial governors and local communities in fiscal, economic, and administrative matters. In fact, the aim of all provincial reform laws, since the first had been enacted in 1864, was to centralize authority in the hands of officials and administrative bodies directly responsible to Istanbul.

Even the realization of his personal dream of election to the *mejlis* was far-fetched. What is known in geographical parlance as Palestine was in fact divided by the Ottomans into three separate administrative units and three separate electoral districts. Areas east of the Jordan river belonged to the *Vilayet* of Damascus. Those territories west of the river and north of a line between Jerusalem and Jaffa were part of the *Vilayet* of Beirut. Most of the Jews resided in the third area, the autonomous *Sanjak* of Jerusalem, south of that same line. Here a Jew did stand a chance to be elected, but only if his coreligionists opted for Ottoman citizenship. This was unlikely, and even if they did, most still belonged to the religious, anti-Zionist community in Jerusalem and would not have voted for a socialist firebrand such as Ben-Gurion.

Nor did Ben-Gurion's visionary plan answer what had come to be known in Zionist jargon as the "Arab question." By Ben-Gurion's own logic, the *Vilayets* of Damascus and Beirut would have been entitled to self-rule, and that self-rule, by his own criteria, would have to be Arab. Did Ben-Gurion mean to hand over these parts of Palestine to Arab control, and leave the Jews—and Zionism—with no more than the autonomous *Sanjak* of Jerusalem? He certainly did not. Although there is no conclusive evidence for the way in which Ben-Gurion resolved this problem, he probably believed that Turkey could be led to grant the Zionist movement all of Palestine as a Jewish autonomous region. This would eventually become a sovereign Jewish state, but in 1914, Ben-Gurion did not believe that he would live to see it established. He had no cause, then, to dwell on the probable fate of the country's Arab inhabitants.

Ben-Gurion did not abandon his Turcophile approach even in the wake of Ottoman crises that he witnessed during his stay in Istanbul. In a short time, as though in a storm, Turkey lost most of its remaining possessions in Africa and Europe in the Tripoli and Balkan wars. Then came the end of hopes for the long-awaited liberty, under the violently installed regime of the Young Turk triumvirate, comprised of Enver, Talat, and Jemal. The Ottoman Empire was in dire straits. Yet the loss of territory only strengthened Ben-Gurion's faith in the "Sick Man." Asiatic Turkey, he argued, would be more homogeneous and hence more stable. Reduced in size and population, and rid of the troublesome Balkan nationalities, Turkey would become a binational empire, essentially Turkish and Arab, bound together by Islam.[5] This should have dispelled his belief that Jews could displace the Arabs as partners of the Turks. Instead, Ben-Gurion and his fellow Jewish classmates in Istanbul launched a round of Turcophile activism.

Shortly after the outbreak of war, the Ottoman government, on September 9, 1914, declared the capitulations abolished. Ben-Gurion, then in Jerusalem for summer vacation, greeted the act enthusiastically, as a freedom-loving Ottoman and a socialist. Although most of Palestine's Jews lamented the move, Ben-Gurion hailed it as "liberation from the chains of servitude to foreign powers." He regarded the abolition of capitulations as a godsend; now the Jews of Palestine would have to become Ottoman citizens and would enjoy the national expression guaranteed them, so Ben-Gurion thought, by the law of the land. Nor was Ben-Gurion deterred by the restrictions placed on Zionist activity following the appointment of Jemal Pasha as commander of the Ottoman Fourth Army, a post that made him virtual dictator over Arabia, Syria, and Palestine. Jemal began a policy of arresting, exiling, and deporting Zionist activists, for fear that they might collaborate with the enemy. Ben-Gurion's response was to plead the Ottoman case still harder and to call on his fellow Jews to show their loyalty. No longer was it sufficient for Jews to declare themselves Ottomans, for many did so simply to avoid expulsion. The true test of Jewish loyalty, in Ben-Gurion's eyes, was willingness to fight for Turkey in the war.

This idea had been raised before, during the Balkan war. At that time, Ben-Gurion's Jewish classmates in the faculty of law, Israel Shochat and Itzhak Ben-Zvi, offered to raise a unit of fifty Jewish cavalrymen to fight in the campaign on the side of Turkey. Enver and Jemal agreed, and Shochat even proceeded to a training base, but by the time the would-be cavalrymen had arrived from Palestine, a cease-fire had been implemented.[6] Now Ben-Gurion and Ben-Zvi revived the idea, and registered in the office of the military commandant of Jerusalem as "volunteers for the Ottoman army." The idea won the approval of the commandant, and the two plunged into the task of organizing a Jewish militia for the defense of Jerusalem. According to Ben-Gurion, one hundred Jews answered an appeal for volunteers published in the party newspaper *Ha'ahdut*. In fact, only about forty persons—including Ben-Gurion, Ben-Zvi, and the editorial and production staff of *Ha'ahdut*—actually began to train with arms. But all these efforts were to no avail. Jemal did not appreciate these gestures of allegiance and disbanded the militia.[7] Yet neither the disbanding of the militia nor the first mass expulsion of Jews in December 1914 dampened Ben-Gurion's Ottoman loyalty. Even Jemal's order for his own and Ben-Zvi's deportation did not erode his faith. On March 23, 1915, Ben-Gurion and Ben-Zvi were taken to Jaffa and put on an Italian ship bound for the port of Alexandria in Egypt. Yet they did not discard the fez, and on arrival in Egypt, they declared to British port officials: "We are Ottomans."

During his incarceration in the Seraya in Jerusalem, prior to his deportation, Ben-Gurion came across Yahya Effendi, an Arab who had studied with him in Istanbul. When Ben-Gurion told Yahya that he was under a deportation order, the Arab replied: "As your friend, I am sorry. As an Arab, I rejoice."[8] In later years, Ben-Gurion would describe this as a dramatic turning point: "This was the first time that I had heard political hostility expressed by an Arab." In his memoirs, Ben-Gurion wrote that at that moment, he saw on the horizon the disturbances that were to rock Palestine.[9]

And so Ben-Gurion himself forgot his speech of October 1910 and his remarks of November 1914, when, mentioning the Arabs, he asked: "Who hates us as they do?" Yet the fact that Ben-Gurion *remembered* Yahya Effendi's remark as a revelation is not without significance. His exchange with Yahya Effendi gave vivid expression to his sense of rivalry with the Arabs for the affection of the power that ruled Palestine. There could be no triangle of constructive cooperation between Jews, Arabs, and that extraneous power. Only one of the two peoples could forge an alliance with the all-powerful third party. That such an alliance was more important to Zionism than any dialogue with the Arabs became an unassailable principle of Ben-Gurion's political doctrine.

Young Ben-Gurion spent the next three years, from May 1915 to May 1918, in the United States. He and Ben-Zvi devoted the early part of their exile to a recruitment campaign for a "pioneer army," known as Hehalutz, and between them they toured thirty-five cities across the continent to win Jewish support for their plan. The two hoped to raise at least 10,000 volunteers who would proceed to Palestine when called and there form "Jewish Legions to fight for Palestine" on Turkey's side. During this campaign, Ben-Gurion set down important principles regarding Jewish and Arab claims. These were spelled out in detail in the first of his articles published in the United States, entitled "Towards the Future."[10]

What fate did the war hold in store for Palestine? Ben-Gurion wrote that "the time has not yet come to discuss the future of Palestine from a broad political point of view. Everything depends upon the outcome of the war, and at this moment, it cannot be forecast with certainty. War is pregnant with surprises." But whatever the outcome, war would be followed by a peace conference, and Ben-Gurion outlined a Jewish strategy for the anticipated talks.

Ben-Gurion's professed aim was a homeland for the Jews in Palestine. He took care not to speak of a state, for that might have been taken by the Turks as incitement to rebellion. This homeland represented the "seed of our aspirations"; it could be borne to fruition by an autonomous, federative, or sovereign Jewish political entity, but the means were secondary to the end. "What we want is not a state of Israel, but the Land of Israel. Our aim is not to dominate but to secure the homeland. . . . what is now within the realm of the possible is clearcut recognition of our right, the right of the Hebrew people, to establish for ourselves a homeland in Palestine." The inevitable peace conference would have to guarantee that right, by ensuring free Jewish immigration and settlement, the right of Jews to participate as equals in the administration of the country, and full communal autonomy.

Did this not represent a threat to the Arab inhabitants of the country? In his article, Ben-Gurion maintained that it did not. The Jews had not come to "dominate and exploit." "We do not intend to push the Arabs aside, to take their land, or to disinherit them." The country was large enough to accommodate both peoples. By Ben-Gurion's calculation, the country had sustained 4 million inhabitants during the last days of the Second Temple, so there was obviously room today for another 3 million or 4 million. Whether or not Ben-Gurion regarded this as an absolute ceiling, he did not say.

To prove his claim that the population could be increased sixfold, Ben-Gurion divided the country into two parts: wilderness, which covered eighty to ninety percent of the land, and inhabited and cultivated tracts. The new Jewish immigrants would settle in the wilderness and make it bloom:

> The land still awaits a cultured and energetic people, rich in spiritual and material resources, armed with modern sci-

> ence and technology; a people to exploit the earth's natural wealth and the country's favorable climate, to irrigate the wasteland, to cause the barren hills to yield fruit, to enrich the abused soil, and to forest the empty sands. Thus will the desert become a Garden of Eden.

But until the desert was made to bloom, the Jews would need arable lands as well. Yet the Arabs need not fear, for such lands would support many more inhabitants:

> Neither does the arable land now yield fruit as it should, because the Arab does not know how to derive the maximum benefit from his labor. The agricultural methods of the Arabs are outmoded and primitive, are ruinous of the soil, and give a poor yield.

The Jews, as they had already proven in their agricultural settlements, would introduce the latest machinery and methods, and improve drainage. Land that once gave forth one sheaf would surrender two or three to the Jews. And again Ben-Gurion spelled out, in detail, the example of Petah-Tikvah. With the help of the Jews, the Arabs too would prosper.

This, then, was the moral justification of Zionism. Far from ruining the Arabs, it would bring them prosperity. "We are building and revitalizing the country," wrote Ben-Gurion, "and this is the *moral and humanitarian basis* of our work of settlement." In this article, Ben-Gurion coined his two mottos: "We will win the land through its reclamation," and "our renewal in this land will come through the renewal of the land itself, and that means the renewal of its Arab inhabitants."

As the war dragged on, and the fate of Palestine hung in the balance, Ben-Gurion turned his thoughts to the dangers and potential windfalls of the outcome, and he put his reflections to paper during a stop in Omaha, Nebraska.[11] The Arab question loomed large in his mind. If Germany and

Turkey emerged victorious, the status quo would be preserved. But what if England and France turned the tide? They might favor Zionist political aims. But there was a danger that "the Catholics might spoil everything," for France was Catholic, and Ben-Gurion still regarded Christian Arabs as the principal foes of Zionism. However, he believed that "we have more to *hope*, in a political sense," from an Allied victory, since the Allies championed democracy and freedom. In any event, it was essential that Zionists in all the warring states prepare themselves, for no matter how the war ended, "the question of Palestine will have to be raised."

Since Ben-Gurion did not foresee the defeat of Germany and the British conquest of Palestine, he continued to prepare for what he regarded as the more realistic prospect of continued Turkish rule. Nor did he believe that a peace conference would deprive even a defeated Turkey of Palestine. And on closer examination, he thought that this might be for the better. After the war, "the Near East will enter upon an era of tremendous development. The Ottoman Empire will stand in need of cultured minds and initiative. Germany will require suitable human resources. The Jews are just such a resource." And now that the Turks were under the gun, "we will use their dire situation to help them, so that they might help us in return." Yet in his Omaha reflections, he was troubled that "the Turks might not understand, or will hold the Arabs of greater account." There was the chance that "the Germans might oppose us" and "a danger that the Arabs might do damage."

For although in his published articles Ben-Gurion denied any conflict between Arab and Jewish interests, he admitted secretly that "yes, there is this certain measure of Arab opposition." "But this can't stop us. First, *we did not come here to expell the Arabs*," but to build. This the Arabs "must understand," for "the Arabs themselves are incapable of such building." Second, "they don't have the power to expell us." Here Ben-Gurion analyzed the reasons for Arab incompetence.

> The Arabs are not organized as a nation and they haven't one national party but many; some want to separate from Turkey while others are satisfied with things as they are, and believe that only tied to Turkey can they develop. But they have no national movement in our sense.

Once the Arabs understood that they were powerless to be rid of the Jews, "then we can work together."

And if they refused? With this possibility in mind, Ben-Gurion advocated the reinforcement of the Yishuv with the volunteers of Hehalutz. In short, Ben-Gurion foresaw armed struggle between Jews and Arabs. "It is possible to come to terms with the Arabs. This is a matter of strategy," he wrote in his Omaha notes. And so it was just as possible, for tactical reasons, not to come to terms. In any event, this was a secondary question, since he believed that the attitude of the power ruling Palestine would determine all.

Disappointed by their recruitment campaign for Hehalutz, Ben-Gurion and Ben-Zvi repaired to writing a book in Yiddish on Palestine. Ben-Gurion sat each day from morning until late evening in the New York Public Library, engrossed in research and writing. In January 1918 the task was finished, and *Palestine, Past and Present* appeared in May.[12] Ben-Zvi contributed the selections on history and geography; Ben-Gurion dealt with political issues, such as borders, territory, administrative divisions, legal systems, and population.

In his chapter on population, Ben-Gurion included a subchapter entitled "The Origin of the Fellah." By examining the history of the Jewish community in Palestine after the destruction of the Second Temple, and analyzing the Arabic names of villages, Ben-Gurion's mind was made up that the fellahs had preserved ancient Jewish traditions through the centuries as well as the place-names cited in the Bible, Talmud, Midrash, and *The Jewish Wars* of Josephus. So greatly did the fellahs venerate and preserve the ancient legacy of their forefathers, that Islamic law was utterly foreign to them, and they still submitted only to their sheikhs. He had no doubt that the fellahs were descendants of the country folk who had inhabited the land at the time of the Arab conquest in the seventh century. In that era, wrote Ben-Gurion, there were "no fewer than a quarter of a million Jews in the country, and quite possibly more," and he believed that he had established the origins of the fellah in this remnant.

Citing the tendency of fellahs to gravitate toward the new Jewish settlements, Ben-Gurion anticipated their eventual "assimilation" into the Yishuv. If this occurred, it was all for the good. The Jewish newcomers, at least in regard to half the population, would not encounter a hostile reception. This analysis fit Ben-Gurion's view of the urban, Christian Arab population as the bitterest foe of Zionism. But even if the fellahs chose to retain their own unique identity, and not be assimilated, the mere fact of their Jewish descent would blunt the hostility of Arabs toward Zionists.

Ben-Gurion's flight of fancy about the assimilation of the fellahs perhaps answered his disappointment in the Jewish agricultural workers then arriving in the country. Many of these were unfit for the rigors of labor in the fields and departed Palestine discouraged and defeated. For a time, Ben-Gurion and others hoped for a solution in the arrival of Jews from Yemen, accustomed as they were to deprivation and hard labor. But they did not arrive in sufficient numbers, and those who came evoked the haughty contempt of other Jews. Ben-Gurion's findings concerning the origins of the fellah offered him an exit from despair. In 1920 he told a visiting delegation of Poalei Zion that

> . . . the most important economic asset of the native population is the fellahs, the builders of the country and its laborers. . . . Under no circumstances must we touch land belonging to fellahs or worked by them. . . . They must receive help from Jewish settlement institutions, to free themselves from their dead weight of their oppressors, and to keep their land. Only if a fellah leaves his place of settlement should we offer to buy his land, at an appropriate price.

And if an effendi landowner sold land worked by fellahs, "then we must give the displaced tenants their own plots, and the means to cultivate such tracts more intensively. When this is impossible, the fellahs must receive new land elsewhere."[13] Ben-Gurion's compassion for the fellah was inspired in part by his socialist convictions, his view of Zionism as a just movement, and his belief that the land belonged to those who actually worked it; but behind all this lingered his firm belief that Jews and fellahs were of the same blood.

3
For Socialist Revolution

The events of 1917 shook the very earth on which Jews stood. The British army, striking out of Egypt, invaded Palestine, and by the close of the year Allenby's soldiers were in Jerusalem. Then came revolution in Russia. So powerful was the impression of events, that Jews imagined themselves on the eve of redemption. But which redemption? Ben-Gurion's colleagues were divided. Some heeded the clarion call of the revolution in Russia and took the first available berth to the new seat of socialism. Others, such as Ben-Gurion and Ben-Zvi, were more enthralled by the prospects of a new Zion, and turned their eyes toward Palestine.

Ben-Gurion regarded the Balfour Declaration as a miracle. "The greatest state in the world has announced its official recognition of the existence of a Hebrew nation, and has committed itself to aid in the establishment of a National Home in Palestine."[1] The question of that homeland's borders, once the preoccupation of historians and Bible scholars, now became a political issue of the first order. The matter was one that the great power in possession of Palestine would settle, and the Zionists could do little more than make representations. In February 1918, a few months after the Balfour Declaration, Ben-Gurion discussed the issue in an article for a New York publication.[2]

After first drawing the necessary distinctions between historical, natural, and demographic borders, Ben-Gurion set aside historical considerations. "The only criteria by which we can draw a line are those determined by nature and the possible extent of settlement." In the north, he thought the demographic factor paramount and intended to exclude densely populated regions from the future Jewish state. "The north of the country is far more populated than the south, and as one approaches Mount Lebanon, the density of settlement increases, and the possibilities for the entry of new masses are much diminished." But with an eye to the future requirements of the Jewish state, Ben-Gurion determined that the water resources of the Litani River were important, and this became his northern border. He noted, too, that Acre and Tyre were the natural entrepôts of this Galilean hinterland, but Sidon "is bound closer to the Lebanon, and is outside the borders of our country."

For the same reason, he drew the northern border at its eastern extremity along the Ouja Wadi, twenty miles south of Damascus.

> It is unthinkable that the Jewish state, in our day and age, could include the city of Damascus. . . . This is a large Arab city, and one of the four centers of Islam. The Jewish community there is small. The Arabs will never allow Damascus their pride, to come under Jewish control, and there can be no doubt that the English, even were it in their power, would never agree to such a thing.

On the other hand, there was a good chance that the southern border might resemble that of Joshua's time. Now that the British had overrun Palestine, Ben-Gurion felt free to discard the prewar frontier between Palestine and Egypt, and argued that "the border runs much further to the south," at

Wadi al-Arish. "Historically, topographically, and geographically, the region of al-Arish is an inseparable part of Palestine, and the division between the region and Turkish Palestine was the result of an arbitrary line drawn by the English and Egyptians between Rafah and Akaba." Ben-Gurion was not precise about this southern border, preferring to regard it as a mobile frontier, to be pushed into the Sinai by the thrust of Jewish settlement. "To the extent that the Jews manage to overcome the obstacles of nature and turn the wasteland into settled country, so the border will shift southwards, and Palestine will extend into Sinai, which is now empty of inhabitants."

Empty spaces in the east also attracted him. "The often-aired opinion, even among Zionists, that Transjordan is not Palestine, rests upon utter ignorance of the history and geography of the country." The eastern border was not the Jordan River, but the Syrian desert, at the furthest edge of Transjordan. This, too, would be a mobile frontier. To secure these empty expanses, Ben-Gurion was prepared to incorporate the populated regions immediately to the east of the Jordan River, a small price to pay for the inclusion of so large a territory, in which "the Hebrew nation was born."

This was the extent of Ben-Gurion's territorial aspirations for what he termed the Jewish "commonwealth," an ambiguous designation that initiates knew to mean a state. His map suited the times. For Ben-Gurion, the war turned the world upside down: regimes fell, new regimes arose from the ruins, empires collapsed, borders were erased, and new states were born. Already in 1915, he began to build his political doctrine on the distinction between static and volatile periods in history. That which might have been unthinkable in settled times could be taken for granted during great upheavals. Such moments had to be exploited. "Now is the hour of unlimited possibilities," he wrote in 1915,[3] and the Balfour Declaration convinced him that the time to strike had arrived. "We have made a sudden leap forward. An arduous road which we had planned to travel slowly and painfully has been shortened and straightened as if by a miracle, and we stand on the threshold of fulfillment," he wrote in November 1917.[4] Ben-Gurion plunged into activity to recruit immigrants and raise funds.

The imminent realization of the Zionist vision demanded that Ben-Gurion clarify his position on the country's Arab inhabitants and do so quickly. What did the future hold in store for this population in a Jewish National Home, commonwealth, or state? Would the Arabs reside there by right or sufferance? Who, indeed, had rights to Palestine?

In laying the moral foundations for possession of Palestine, Ben-Gurion did not emphasize the historical rights of a people to the land of its ancient forefathers. Either he did not think it a sufficient claim, or preferred to balance it with two other claims that he held to be of equal importance.

The first of these was the right established by Jewish need. In 1915 he wrote that Palestine was the only country that could relieve the misery of the Jews: "The solution for any homeless people should and must be a *homeland* in its historical birthplace."

But of equal weight was the right earned by creativity and work, the conviction that a land belongs to those willing and able to develop it. Not only the Arabs had a right to Palestine, but so did the Jewish people, who could not be denied the right to labor in the land of their forefathers. Specifically, the Arabs had rights to those lands on which they lived and which they cultivated. But since they "are incapable of reviving the land and restoring it from ruin," and cultivated only some twenty percent of its territory, the Jews had the full right to settle on the remnant, to make the desert bloom by the sweat of their brows, and to make their homes a homeland.[5]

Ben-Gurion borrowed his guiding principles on this issue

from John Locke and Karl Marx; idleness was a sin, purposeful activity was a commandment. Building, planting, improving yields, exploiting natural resources—man had the right to pursue any kind of activity destined to secure his material prosperity. The right of the Jews to the land rested on their capacity for developing it. For many years, this was his principal claim, and he carried it to some extremes. In 1930 he declared:

> We do not recognize any form of absolute ownership over any country. Any group of diligent persons, every industrious people, is entitled to enjoy the fruits of labor, and do with its talents as it pleases. It has no right to prevent others from doing the same, or to close the doors leading to nature's gifts in the faces of others. The five million inhabitants of Australia have no right to close the gates of their continent—which they alone cannot fully exploit—and so exclude the masses of desperate people seeking a new place to work. This is the principle behind the right of free migration, championed by international socialism.[6]

Ben-Gurion thus regarded the freedom to settle in empty spaces as a natural and moral right, and one that supported the Jewish claim to Palestine.

To what extent did the Arab population of Palestine share that right? Ben-Gurion was never very precise on that question. At least in theory, he conferred on the Arabs the same rights as the Jews. The Arabs had such rights as stemmed from history and their own industriousness. And since they had inhabited the land "for hundreds of years,"[7] and had cultivated and built on it, their right to continue to do so could not be doubted. In an article devoted especially to this subject, entitled "The Rights of Jews and Others in Palestine," he set down this principle: "Palestine is not an empty country . . . *on no account must we injure the rights of its inhabi-*

tants."[8] Ben-Gurion often returned to this point, emphasizing that the Arabs had "the full right" to an independent economic, cultural, and communal life.[9]

But Ben-Gurion set limits. The Arabs, themselves incapable of developing the country, had no right to stand in the way of the Jews. In 1918, he determined that rights sprang not from the past but from the future,[10] and in 1924 he declared: "We do not recognize the right of Arabs to rule the country, since Palestine is still undeveloped and awaits its builders."[11] The Arabs were not entitled to control or prohibit this constructive activity. In 1928 he pronounced that "the Arabs have no right to close the country to us. What right do they have to the Negev desert, which is uninhabited?";[12] and in 1930, "The Arabs have no right to the Jordan river, and no right to prevent the construction of a power plant [by a Jewish concern]. They have a right only to that which they have created and to their own homes."[13] The rights of the Arabs were valid, then, only in their confined places of residence. They could, of course, settle in the empty expanses as well, but because of their economic underdevelopment, it was obvious that they would not. In Ben-Gurion's mind, they were incapable of it.

A more serious limitation arose from Ben-Gurion's unwillingness to regard the Arabs of Palestine as a people in their own right. During the Ottoman period, the country north of a line between Jerusalem and Jaffa had been part of the *Vilayets* of Damascus and Beirut. The Arabs of the country had regarded themselves as part of southern Syria. Even after the British occupation, they did not see themselves as a separate national entity. Ben-Gurion, like many of his generation, thought of all the Arabs of the Near East as one great people of many millions. In contrast to the homeless Jews, the Arab people had many homelands. In 1929 he said in an unequivocal manner that

> Jerusalem is not the same thing to the Arabs as it is to the Jews. The Arab people inhabits many great lands, whose territory in Asia alone equals a third of Europe. . . . But for the Jewish people—in every generation and place of dispersion—Palestine is the one and only country with which its national destiny has been tied.[14]

The sum of this reasoning was that the Arabs of Palestine were entitled only to autonomy. In 1918 Ben-Gurion stated that "the national-religious communities of Palestine should be guaranteed full internal autonomy in all cultural, economic and social affairs."[15] But future sovereignty would be the portion of the Jews alone.

Finally there was his socialist conviction. The aim of socialism, as a just movement, was to divide everything equally, not only among individuals, but among nations. As the Arabs had many lands, and the Jews had lost their only one, it was obvious that justice dictated the restoration of Palestine to the Jews. Furthermore, the socialist awakening that followed the Russian Revolution—and in Ben-Gurion's opinion was soon to sweep the Middle East—would open the eyes of the Arabs to the justice of a Jewish Palestine and the two blessings conferred on the country by socialist Zionism: development and revolution. In Ben-Gurion's mind, socialism was the road to the heart of the Arab people, in Palestine and elsewhere. And "we must find a reliable road . . . we must win the trust of the Arabs in the Jewish people."[16]

In linking his Zionism to socialism, Ben-Gurion entered a labyrinth of contradictions. Socialism demanded an equal division of all resources, without regard for religion, nationality, or race; and did not the needs of hundreds of thousands of Arabs come before those of the few Jewish immigrants? Yet Zionism was sworn to devote most if not all of its energies to the immigration and absorption of Jews. How could the socialist vision of peace among nations be realized, when

Zionism stood for separate Jewish status and claimed the lion's share of the country's resources? If the aim of socialism was peace among nations, did Jewish immigration not represent a stumbling block, since it aggravated relations between Jews and Arabs?

Ben-Gurion was not blind to the contradictions. But his inability to resolve them did not lead him to abandon his problem-ridden combination of Zionism and socialism. To his mind, this lame solution was better than other partial solutions, free of internal contradictions but unfair to the Arabs, and hence immoral. Ben-Gurion apparently preferred the ambiguities of Zionist socialism to anti-Zionist socialism or antisocialist Zionism, with their comprehensive and irrefutable arguments. Ben-Gurion's assumption was that the difficulties would be resolved in the future, once the inevitable wave of socialism swept through the Middle East. In the meantime, it was essential to pour water and not oil on the flames—to deny a conflict of interests between Jews and Arabs, and so win supporters for Labor Zionism. Did it ever occur to him that the future might not fulfill his promises? If it did, he never made the slightest allusion to his doubts.

The Comintern was less sanguine. During the fifth world conference of Poalei Zion, held in Vienna in August 1920, the prospect of membership in the Comintern forced the party to clarify its attitude toward Zionism.[17] Ben-Gurion maintained on that occasion that Zionism and socialism were complementary, that Zionist socialists were not anomalies and did not differ in essence from German or British socialists. The only distinction that he was prepared to admit was this one: "The task of other socialists is primarily political—to seize power and remake their national economy into a socialist one. But we must first build an economy, and root it in socialist principles. Our principal task is one of constructing," not remaking.

Ben-Gurion did not reject membership in the Comintern,

but he had certain reservations. It was important that the Jews not be made the victims of revolution in Palestine, as they had been in Russia. "And we cannot blindly obey" the Comintern, because it supported the "Feisals" and "the rest of the imperialist effendis." World revolution would best be served by the establishment of a socialist, Hebrew nation in Palestine, which then could disseminate the gospel throughout the neighboring countries. Later he would embrace the criticisms made by Nahman Syrkin: "Lenin is attempting to be a realistic politician, and the sympathy of Arabs in Syria and Egypt, notorious for their hatred of Zionism, is more important to him than the growth of the Jewish community in Palestine. Lenin is sacrificing the Hebrew people on the altar of world revolution." When it came to other nations and peoples, Ben-Gurion was a communist who argued for dictatorship of the proletariat, and even declared that "I am for Bolshevism." But when it came to the Jewish people and Palestine, Ben-Gurion championed the dictatorship of Zionism.

But if the Comintern was prepared to admit a Zionist party—and so far it was not—Ben-Gurion would join. If membership could be of some use in securing the return of the Jewish people to their land and Jewish independence, he favored it. And he recognized the tremendous power wielded by Russia. He was convinced that "we must conduct a dialogue with Russia's leaders," in order "to explain to them the nature of true Zionism." For that purpose he would travel to Moscow in 1923; until 1928 he continued to believe that by a careful presentation, he might lead the masters of the Kremlin and the Comintern to recognize the legitimate cause of Labor Zionism.

At the same time, Ben-Gurion came to believe that Labor Zionism would have a truly liberating impact on Palestine and the Middle East. In 1921, Ben-Gurion proposed to a conference of Ahdut Ha'avodah that Jewish and Arab workers cooperate in every field; this was a precondition for the "redemption" of the Jewish people and "the liberation of the working Arab people from subservience to its oppressors," the landowners. The "historic mission" of the Jewish worker in Palestine was "to stand at the vanguard of the movement of liberation and revival of Near Eastern peoples."[18] In 1925 he told the Zionist Congress: "Our Zionist enterprise cannot and must not oppose those forces which, tomorrow or the next day, will determine the destiny of the entire world and Palestine. This force is the working class, soon to come to power . . . our activity in this direction corresponds to the thrust of world history." And so the Jewish people "cannot succeed without participating in the great movement of awakening that stirs the peoples of the East to political and cultural rebirth . . . and foremost among them are the Arabs."[19] In 1927, in addressing the third conference of the General Labor Federation (Histadrut), Ben-Gurion declared that the masses of Jewish workers who would arrive in Palestine would "strengthen the hand of the Arab workers and masses in Palestine and neighboring countries." Whether Jewish workers numbered 30,000, or 300,000, or 3 million Arabs would not be displaced. To the contrary: "When we become a great force, we can help the Arab workers, and raise up the Arab masses from their degradation. We will be a tremendous factor in the blossoming of these countries."[20]

It was impossible to shake Ben-Gurion from his belief in the liberating and beneficial mission of Labor Zionism. Total rejection by the Comintern, criticism by colleagues and opponents, and even the bloody disturbances of 1920 and 1921, in which the Arabs vented their hostility to Zionism and the imposition of the Mandate, left him unmoved. His unshakable adherence to the socialist solution of Jewish–Arab conflict drew strength from need—his need to see Zionism as just. For only in a socialist world could Palestine be secured as a homeland, and then as a state, by peaceful agreement.

But Ben-Gurion did not propose to postpone realization of the Zionist vision until the arrival of the revolutionary millennium. In November 1917 he declared that "within the next twenty years, we must have a Jewish majority in Palestine."[21] By his calculation, a million Jews had to arrive by 1938 to meet his target. From the outset, he built his program on the principle that there was no conflict of interests between Jew and Arab. To prevent friction and dispute, his idea was to physically distance the assets of the future, which the Jews were to build, from the existing assets in possession of the country's Arabs. For fear that the issue might open a Pandora's box, Ben-Gurion even excluded the holy places and houses of prayer from a restored Zion: "This is non-Jewish territory," he wrote in 1918, "over which the authority derived from the sovereign rights of the Hebrew people will not be exercised."[22]

Ben-Gurion placed the work of renewal in the desert and the wastelands. He told a visiting delegation in 1920 that the possibilities for massive settlement of Jews lay in the abandoned or uninhabited reaches—including, of course, those across the Jordan—on land that had no owners, and on partially utilized tracts owned privately or by the government. He estimated that four fifths of the country's territory was available for new settlement.[23] Six million persons using modern methods could earn their livelihoods from farming these lands; an untold number could prosper from industry.[24] None of this activity would impinge on the Arabs, who would continue to live in their established areas, while Jews lived in new settlements and worked new fields. Contact, and friction, between the two peoples would thus be reduced to a minimum.

It was now that Ben-Gurion began to call for a segregation of labor. In 1906 he had accepted the employment of Arabs at Petah-Tikvah as a fact of life; in 1907 he called for the exclusive employment of Jews only on lands owned by the

Jewish National Fund. But now he became uncompromising in his insistence that Jews employ only Jews. His was a position rooted in the conviction that the Jewish people in Palestine must be made a productive people; the Jew had to be transformed and made creative. "This is not a means but a sublime end." Only in this manner could the Jewish economy expand and accommodate still more immigrants. For Ben-Gurion's dreams of a massive influx of Jews were haunted by two specters. The first was the fear that Jewish capitalist development would favor cheap Arab labor. "On all the farms established on a private capitalist basis, most of the workers are not Jews."[25] The second was his apprehension over Arab hatred that was liable to spring from such exploitation. Hence, his belief that "Arab labor must not be exploited by Jewish capital. The Jewish people must create its own new economy through Jewish labor."[26]

And so Jews and Arabs, separated by religion and culture, would live in separate settlements and work in separate economies. Only in one field would there be mixed labor: in public works and government service. By this division into two national entities, Ben-Gurion sought to lay the foundation of a partition of the country into two autonomous frameworks, Jewish and Arab. The idea of partition had struck him even before his arrival in the country. In the 1920s he would speak repeatedly of the "total equality of the two peoples and their independence in internal affairs,"[27] and of his program for two autonomes.

The aid that Jews would extend to Arabs on the path to progress and social liberation would start with the working class. The Histadrut, as a separate Jewish national federation, would help to create a separate Arab labor federation. The two federations would be linked "in a covenant of brotherhood, truth, and equality."[28] Only in public works and government service, in which Jew and Arab worked side by side, was there justification for shared labor federations. The first joint federation—and ultimately the only one—was the railway workers union, which the Histadrut established. The general Jewish federation would extend every aid to the general Arab federation; the Jewish worker would demonstrate to the Arab worker how to stand tall and organize. Together, the two national federations would form a front of Palestinian workers, within which both federations would enjoy absolute autonomy. And together they would work to organize Arab workers in neighboring countries.[29] Upon their conversion to socialism, "the Arabs will welcome us with open arms, or at least will reconcile themselves to our growth and independence."[30]

4

The Denial Begins

In August 1918, Ben-Gurion arrived in Egypt as a volunteer in one of the Jewish battalions destined for Palestine. An Allied victory was now inevitable; Ben-Gurion, admitting his miscalculation, put on a British uniform. He was stationed at Tel el-Kebir, in the desert halfway between Ismailia and Cairo. Shortly after his arrival, the battalion was joined by volunteers from Palestine, among them Berl Katznelson. In the fashion of a conspiracy, they founded Ahdut Ha'avodah (United Labor), which comprised most of Poalei Zion and the nonpartisan agricultural workers under the leadership of Katznelson, Itzhak Tabenkin, and David Remez. Their secret aim was the creation of a socialist Jewish state; their professed aim was the establishment of a "workers' commonwealth." It was too early in the day to demand a state, for in all of Palestine on both banks of the Jordan there were only 58,000 Jews and over a million Arabs. Clearly Zionism's first task had to be the creation of a Jewish majority through large-scale immigration and settlement. In the moment of enthusiasm that followed the armistice, Zionists expected a wave of mass immigration, reaching at least 200,000 in the first few years. These hopes were soon dashed, and in 1931 Palestine's Jews numbered only 174,600. But in the halcyon days following the war, expectations still ran high, and Zionist minds were too preoccupied to give thought to the place of the Arabs in the future "workers' commonwealth."

It was not that the leaders and members of Ahdut Ha'avodah ignored the Arabs; they were more conscious of the issue than many others, but they approached it strictly from the angle of defense. The Arabs posed a problem of security to Jewish settlements; the response of Ahdut Ha'avodah was to establish the Haganah (self-defense) in July 1920. For as early as 1918, the Arabs had begun to organize against the implementation of the Balfour Declaration. In 1919, Tabenkin observed that "suspicious signs are becoming more evident daily" of an impending massacre and that "our slaughter has been made too easy." The Haganah was born not in anticipation of such an eventuality, but in its wake. From late 1919, Arab attacks on Jewish settlements became more frequent and relentless, particularly in the Jordan Valley and the Galilee. In 1920, the outpost of Tel-Hai fell, and with it Joseph Trumpeldor and seven of his fellow defenders. The event inscribed a new chapter in Zionist national hagiography and heroism. At the same time, trouble spread to the cities, and in April 1920, riot reigned in Jerusalem for two days, leaving six Jews dead, two hundred wounded, and three hundred homeless. The force of the Arab protest, and the failure of the British military administration to enact preventive measures, stunned Jews and Zionists throughout the world. The violence in Jerusalem seemed a pogrom in all but name, one which would have made Czarist Russia's greatest Jew-haters proud. The Allied decision taken in San Remo, to install Great Britain as the mandatory in Palestine, brought little respite. In 1921 the demonstrations and agitation began again, and in May the bloodshed spread to Jaffa and its suburbs. The consequences were far more serious than those of the previous year's violence. Jewish dead numbered 47; 116 were wounded. This time the British army put down the disturbances forciably but late. Jewish immigration was suspended for a time, until Arab tempers had cooled. The next eight years were quiet ones for Palestine, but the Arab national movement had proved its ability to mobilize the masses, lead them to riot, and bring immigration to a halt.

How did the theoreticians of Ahdut Ha'avodah interpret these events? It was usual for them to describe the Arab demonstrators and rioters as wildmen and thieves. Tabenkin spoke of "the frenzied masses and Arab robbers" who were assaulting Jews "without fear."[1] Menahem Ussishkin said that "thieves are ambushing us."[2] Berl Katznelson, in describing the Jerusalem violence, wrote of the "knife-stabs of the vile mob, wild and incited."[3] In other words, the riots were the outgrowth of a clash between two cultures—one, uncivilized and born of the desert, aggressive and treacherous; the other, that of farmers and peaceful citizens. The references to thieves gave the agitation a criminal character. This was not to cast aspersions on all the Arabs of Palestine. But the degradation of certain individual Arabs was highlighted by the contrast with their victims, who were virtually canonized. The author Yosef-Haim Brenner—who was himself murdered in the 1921 violence—described Trumpeldor as "the symbol of pure heroism" who fell at the hands of "the perverse."[4] Whether the leaders of Ahdut Ha'avodah detested the Arabs as a collective will never be known. They were usually reticent about making general statements on the Arabs and did not publicly air their views. A striking example was Berl Katznelson's *Yizkor*, compiled in homage to the fallen of Tel-Hai. He did not even hint at the Arab identity of the enemy in that "fierce battle," which claimed Tel-Hai's heroic defenders.[5]

Still another approach favored by the members of Ahdut Ha'avodah was evident in their virulent campaign against the British military administration and its leading figures. Katznelson and Tabenkin wrote that the riots were the handiwork of the military government, and made special mention of Chief Administrator Lt. General Sir Louis Jean Bols, and Governor of Jerusalem Sir Ronald Storrs. Then there was the Marxist or class analysis of the violence, advocated by the socialists of Ahdut Ha'avodah. The "frenzied" Arabs obviously had been incited against the Jews by the "effendis." Ben-Zion Israeli maintained that "the effendis and Arab notables, those who live off exploiting the masses and enforce the grimest servitude, are directing a campaign of violence against us."[6] So prevalent was the class interpretation that even its most glaring inconsistencies went unnoticed. Moshe Sharett's article on an anti-Zionist demonstration held in Jaffa on February 27, 1920, provided a remarkable example.[7] Sharett gave a good account of the demonstration but went to great lengths to distinguish between the organizers—"outside instigators," "the clergy," and "the effendis"—and the crowd who participated. "The Arab crowd did not impress one as being excited or demonstrative, but seemed more like a curious audience gathered to view a play staged to entertain them." Yet Sharett had opened the very same article with a description of the widespread participation in a general strike: "Arab workshops and offices were closed from the morning. Arab artisans and workers were on strike. The dockworkers refused to unload the cargo of a ship in Jaffa port. On the doors of the shut shops were printed handbills: 'Closed in protest against the idea of making Palestine a Jewish National Home.' " Had these Arabs forfeited their wages and profits for a cause with which they did not identify, simply to satisfy "outside agitators"? Such were the intellectual gymnastics necessitated by the need to believe that the Arab opponents of Zionism were but an evil minority.

The British military government did not share this opinion. From the outset, British intelligence officers reported widespread and popular Arab opposition to the Balfour Declaration, immigration, the National Home policy, and the British mandate installed to enforce them. As early as 1919, Storrs wrote to his superiors in Cairo that the Arabs opposed Zionism, and warned the chief political officer of the Egyptian Expeditionary Force, Sir Gilbert Clayton, that anti-Zionist propaganda had so increased that riots against the Jews were likely in Jaffa and elsewhere. In his opinion, the granting of special privileges to Jews was bound to result in disorder, despite the military government's precautions.[8] Reports submitted by British intelligence and political officers soon brimmed with accounts of anti-Zionist sentiment and Arab attempts to give the hostility an organized expression. At the same time, investigations of certain Zionist groups created a profound British apprehension that the immigrant Jew bore the seeds of Bolshevik revolution. In this view, it was the Jews who were the unsettling element in an increasingly volatile mix.

This set the stage for a bitter contest between the Zionists and the military government. Their analyses of the disturbances could not have been further apart. Ahdut Ha'avodah and other Zionist circles claimed that the violence was the work of "mischief-makers" who incited and instigated the mob. The military government and the Arabs held that the violence expressed a genuine opposition to Zionism shared by most if not all Arabs, who feared they would be deprived of their land by the National Home and dispossessed of their culture by imported Bolshevism. Already in 1919, officers of the military administration had come to identify themselves with the Arab cause, arguing that a Jewish National Home could be bought only at the price of Arab violence. The Zionists regarded this as a self-fulfilling expectation and blamed the disturbances on the British. In April 1920, in the wake of the Jerusalem violence, the Provisional Council of Palestine Jewry cabled London: "The entire Jewish community is endangered by this administration, which bears responsibility for this pogrom."[9] Ahdut Ha'avodah's condemnation was even more severe, for it demanded that Bols and Storrs be put on trial. Katznelson spoke of a "political pogrom."[10] Tabenkin went still further: "This government has declared open war against the Jews."[11] The charge ran into difficulty after July 1920, when the military government was replaced by a civil administration under High Commissioner Sir Herbert Samuel, a Jew and a Zionist. When more Jewish blood was spilt in 1921, the Zionists would not demand Samuel's removal as they had his predecessor's.

Although there was no doubt that the military government came to oppose Zionism, British officers did not manufacture Arab opposition to Zionism.[12] They may at times have attempted to use such opposition to British advantage, but they did not organize anti-Zionist sentiment. The military administration's policy did not aim to settle the differences between Jews and Arabs but could not be accused of creating those differences. Yet Ahdut Ha'avodah chose to ignore this fact. In 1920 and 1921, the party was not prepared to admit what every officer in the military administration knew for a fact: that the roots of opposition to Zionism had struck deep in the hearts of Palestine's Arabs and had grown thick. The attitude of Ahdut Ha'avodah, and of wider Zionist circles, too, was one of plain denial.

Ben-Gurion had remarkably little to say about the violent events of 1920 and 1921. As the moving spirit in the Ahdut Ha'avodah secretariat, his professed interpretation was in line with that of his colleagues. "Wildmen" and "thieves" perpetrated the attacks, and responsibility rested with the British military administration. The latter had given the Arabs the sense that the government stood by them, expressed in the slogan chanted by the rioters: *ad-dawla ma'ana*, "the government is with us." The disbanding of the Jewish battalions and the ban on immigration were at the root of this evil. Both measures weakened the Yishuv and emboldened the Arabs.

Without them, Tel-Hai would not have fallen, and the Galilean settlements would not have been abandoned.[13] Here were the origins of Ben-Gurion's later conviction that a large and strong Yishuv would bring peace to Palestine, since the Arabs would despair of eliminating it.

In the name of Ahdut Ha'avodah, Ben-Gurion entered the fray in an attempt to bring about the dismissal of the military government by impassioned appeals to world public opinion. "The Arabs intend to wipe out the Jewish settlements," he wrote in long letters and cables to newspapers in America and Europe, to the British Labor Party and to Poalei Zion branches. "If we do not fortify our settlements in time, and add thousands of working hands to the Yishuv, that which happened in the Upper Galilee might well befall us here."[14] In a cable to the London *Daily Herald*, which was published in full, Ben-Gurion demanded the removal of Bols and Storrs, who were responsible for the pogrom in Jerusalem.[15] One of the aims of his mission to London was to influence public opinion, especially within the Labor Party, to bring about the recall of leading figures in the military administration. He set out on his journey in June 1920.

All that Ben-Gurion had said on Tel-Hai and the riot in Jerusalem, he had said in the collective name of Ahdut Ha'avodah. He was always careful to distinguish between first-person singular and first-person plural—between his own views and those of the party for which he spoke. And he, who seethed with ideas, reactions, and comments on every Zionist subject imaginable, kept his silence on the most pressing issue of all. There is nothing that bears his name concerning the events of 1920. Even the accusatory declaration of Ahdut Ha'avodah's executive committee,[16] which blamed the military administration for the Jerusalem riot, was written not by Ben-Gurion but by Ben-Zvi's brother. This was quite unusual, as Ben-Gurion always wrote party statements in his own hand. In fact, Ben-Gurion, alone among Ahdut

Ha'avodah's leading lights, did not write so much as a word on the blood spilt at Tel-Hai and Jerusalem. Was he of two minds about the issue, unable to decide whether to openly blame Arab nationalism, thus making public his awareness of the real root of the conflict?

While still abroad, Ben-Gurion learned of the recurrence of violence in May 1921, and he was horrified. On July 29, 1921, he returned to Jaffa by the first ship to deboard Jewish newcomers after the lifting of the three-month immigration ban. As was customary in those days, he went from ship to shore in an Arab-manned skiff, along with six other Jews. Ben-Gurion searched the faces of the eight Arab oarsmen for any sign of hostility toward the Jewish passengers, and he noted their every movement and inflection. He breathed easy—no sign of tension. Ben-Gurion did not detect in the sailors "any sign of bitterness which afflicts a man forced to do something against his own will." In the port, he found that nothing had changed. "The Arabs look as they did yesterday and the day before," he wrote to his father. Arab hatred was not as pervasive as some made it out to be. In talking with colleagues from Ahdut Ha'avodah, he learned that the quiet that prevailed in Jaffa was the handiwork of the tough new governor, Major James Campbell. Ben-Gurion immediately drew the conclusion that Herbert Samuel had erred in banning immigration to appease the Arabs. "Now I have seen with my own eyes what the 'Jewish High Commissioner' is liable to do to us out of cowardice and weakness," he wrote to friends abroad.[17]

The anniversary of the Balfour Declaration provided Arab leaders with another opportunity to display their opposition to the National Home policy. Their plan was to make November 2, 1921, a day of national mourning, marked by strikes and demonstrations. The governors of the Jaffa and Haifa districts prohibited demonstrations and placed the army on alert. But Storrs, the governor of Jerusalem, took no such precautions; he attempted to speak to the hearts of the Arab demonstrators. They cheered him, some even hoisted him on their shoulders—and then they lit out for the Jewish quarter to riot and pillage. Five Jews were killed by the mob.

Ben-Gurion finally broke his silence, for the only time in the two unsettled years of violence, and published a reaction in his own name. He came out in support of his party's stand, denying the existence of a national conflict. In an article entitled "Whose Hand Has Shed the Blood?," he repeated the well-known litany of Ahdut Ha'avodah.[18] The Arab rioters were "wildmen" and "thieves" manipulated by agitators, and the authorities were at fault. He wrote with an air of authority about the character of the Arabs: "By now we are familiar with the people of this country. We know their manner. We have heard of and seen many instances of robbery and murder. We have witnessed incidents and clashes, and those with a destructive bent do not discriminate between stranger and kinsman." In other words, it was the way of the Arabs to rob and quarrel, both among themselves and with others. What had happened was not an expression of anti-Zionism or hatred of Jews. "There was never a pogrom under Turkish rule, so notorious for its degeneracy, impotence and incompetence. . . . That government, though anti-Zionist, did not want pogroms, and there were none." Since the pogroms began only after the British occupation, Ben-Gurion was led to conclude that it was not the Arabs collectively who were to blame, but "human scum" manipulated by "open and covert agitators, evil plot-hatchers, and wicked administrators"—the officers of the military government. They were responsible for the bloody Passover of 1920, and "their sentence is to descend from the throne."

Indeed, the military government had been replaced although for different reasons. But Samuel was to blame for not having deposed *all* of the "official agitators" from his civilian government, who continued to inflame war between

Jews and Arabs. The most notorious of them was Storrs, leader of the "evil, blood-stained" officers. Little wonder that the pogrom occurred in Jerusalem under his governance. To his question, "on whose hands is the Jewish blood shed for a second time in Jerusalem?" Ben-Gurion answered with the name of Storrs, "successor to Pontius Pilate." Ben-Gurion called for his immediate removal.

In essence, Ben-Gurion's criticisms singled out but one man. Had Storrs been dismissed earlier, the pogrom never would have happened. Ben-Gurion made no mention of the origins of Arab unrest. He spoke only of its consequences, the bloodshed. Yet if the Turkish period had been one of peace, was it not because the Arabs had not then felt threatened by the Jews? Now the Jews were to have a National Home, and the country was ruled by a Jew and Zionist. That was how the Arabs themselves explained their opposition. If so simple and obvious a conclusion eluded Ben-Gurion, did this not prove that he was a prisoner of an interpretation spun by himself, that he saw only what he wished to see?

This was not necessarily so. Had his ideas been fixed, he would not have waited two years to express them, but would have lent his voice to the clamor of his colleagues in Ahdut Ha'avodah. But he was a political man, much more so than the others. Ben-Gurion would have made a political calculation before settling on a public interpretation, with the welfare of the Yishuv in mind. Would he have chosen Jabotinsky's blunt approach, and declared that "a voluntary settlement between us and the Arabs in Palestine is unthinkable, now and in the foreseeable future"? To posit an irreconcilable conflict in this manner would have harmed the prospects of the Yishuv, for it would have deepened Arab hatred and could have cost the Jews the sympathy of world public opinion. No one was prepared to impose the Jews on the Arabs by brute force with Wilsonian talk of self-determination in the air. Ben-Gurion rejected Jabotinsky's demand for an "Iron Wall," that is, that only under the shield of an armed force could Zionism achieve its aim.[19] In that event, and in the absence of a Jewish armed force, the British army would have to defend the Yishuv against implacable foes. But Ben-Gurion maintained that the land could not be won by reliance on others.

"The homeland cannot be given as a gift," wrote Ben-Gurion. "It cannot be purchased like a concession through political contracts, bought with gold, or seized by force. The land can be earned only by building, by the sweat of one's brow."[20] Ben-Gurion was not blind to what Jabotinsky saw; he already had written of the depth of Arab hatred for Zionism. But to reiterate this point and inscribe it as a principle of Zionist doctrine would have been pointless. He preferred a positive and beneficial tactic, one that burned no bridges and left open a chance for peace, however remote. It is difficult to establish Ben-Gurion's considerations with assurance, since his tactical denial of the real conflict had to be total to be convincing. In 1939, Ben-Gurion confessed that he often took positions on the Arab question for tactical reasons, and not out of conviction.[21] This might well have been such an instance.

Ben-Gurion made it the policy of Ahdut Ha'avodah never to refuse dialogue with three great forces: Great Britain, world socialism, and the Arabs. Immediately after his return from London, he began once again to speak of cooperation between Jewish and Arab workers. While the Yishuv was still reeling from the violence of May 1921, he published a proposal entitled "Relations with Our Neighbors."[22] His timing bordered on the insensitive, for memories of Tel-Hai and the tragedies of the past two years were so many open wounds. Yet this is what Ben-Gurion wrote:

> The establishment of comradely relations between Hebrew workers and the masses of Arab laborers, grounded in common economic, political and cultural action is an essential

> condition for our redemption as a working people, and the liberation of the working Arab people from servitude to propertied oppressors. The task of laying the groundwork for common action belongs to the Hebrew worker . . . who must stand at the vanguard of the movement of liberation and reawakening of Near Eastern peoples.

What could be the first step? The Jewish General Labor Federation founded in December 1920—the Histadrut—soon would open a Public Works Office, which would bid on government construction and road-building contracts. Histadrut projects carried out under such contracts would employ "mixed labor, Arab and Hebrew workers." The Arabs would be employed by the Histadrut Public Works Office at salaries and conditions identical to those of Jewish workers.

Ben-Gurion continued to believe as always in segregated labor organization, and he did not propose that the Histadrut represent the Arabs it employed. Instead, its Public Works Office and representatives of the Arab workers would establish a joint directorate. The directorate would establish a sick fund for the Arabs, affiliated with the Histadrut sick fund. It would operate kitchens affiliated with the Histadrut's food cooperative. The directorate would also organize cultural activities: "The leisure time of the Arab workers will be occupied with informal and easy lectures about the labor movement, collective life, Arab and general history, hygiene, etc." "The principal aim of this cooperative activity must be to educate the Arab worker to organized labor, to imbue him with a sense of discipline and responsibility for his fellow workers."

Ben-Gurion had returned from London more a socialist than ever. Socialist revolution was just around the corner; all that was needed to turn that corner was a helpful nudge. When one considers that Ben-Gurion advocated at this time that the entire Histadrut be made a commune, his plan for cooperation with Arab workers comes into sharper relief. Nor was his attitude to the Arab worker condescending. Ben-Gurion held that socialism faced a still more difficult task in transforming the Jews from "rootless parasites to productive workers." Once installed as secretary of the Histadrut, Ben-Gurion set about implementing his bold vision of cooperation.

5
Workers, Unite?

In November 1921, Ben-Gurion was elected to the Executive Committee of the Histadrut. Although he was but one of the members, he soon established himself as the committee's all-powerful secretary. For the next fifteen years, the Histadrut provided the principal outlet for his energies. Now he was in a position to bring all of his talents to bear on promotion of a cooperative relationship with Arab workers.

The executive committee had grappled with the issue for some time. The crux of the problem concerned the organizational framework for cooperation. The communists had a clear solution, for they simply advocated the creation of a united labor federation embracing both Arabs and Jews. But division by nationality was a fundamental principle of the Histadrut, which had been established as a federation of "Hebrew workers." Arab workers, in the Histadrut's concept, were to be organized in their own unions. But should the Arab workers then be left to their own devices, or should the Histadrut play an active role and assist them? Tabenkin held that "if we don't maintain ties with them, they will oppose us." But Israel Shochat opposed all assistance, believing that the Arabs would use their federation to mobilize anti-Zionist sentiment. "They'll learn the best organizational techniques, and will turn them against us." He believed that once the Arabs had established their federation on their own—a doubtful prospect—then "certainly we can find a way to link with them."[1] A consensus on this issue seemed beyond reach.

The main arguments against Ben-Gurion's vision of cooperation were spelled out in an article by a rank-and-file member of the Histadrut.[2] "Who is going to undertake this? We? Ninety-nine percent of us don't even know how to properly greet an Arab whom we meet in the street. Their mannerisms and customs are strange to us, as are their ways of thinking. Are we up to the task? And if we also consider the sorry state of our relations with the Arabs, their distrust in us which various effendis have managed to instill in them, and their blind obedience to their leaders, then the picture is complete." In any case, were Jewish workers in so enviable a state that the Histadrut could afford to squander its resources on strangers? Most of the Jewish labor unions were foundering. Was it really the historic mission of the Hebrew worker to bring revolution to the Middle East? "Not a single worker came to this country, with the possible exception of a few recent arrivals, with this 'historic mission' in mind." First, let us fortify our own positions. In the various cooperative schemes, the author saw "a threat to our endeavor in this country."

Such criticisms did not dampen Ben-Gurion's enthusiasm, and he began to lecture in public on "Relations with Our Neighbors." Once elected to the Histadrut Executive Committee, he dispelled the mist of confusion that surrounded the issue. Ben-Gurion saw the task before him clearly: the establishment of an Arab labor federation was essential to Labor Zionism, both for educational and practical political reasons. But before he could act, he needed the sanction of the Histadrut Council, which was scheduled to meet in January 1922 and had managed to avoid any straightforward decision on the Arabs on every previous occasion. Ben-Gurion employed a surprise tactic to ensure that the issue was not shunted aside again. He presented a draft resolution for vote in the closing session, leaving no time for debate; but by way of preparation, he had published his arguments in his party organ.[3]

Ben-Gurion's case was this: the low wage of the unorganized Arab worker, whose needs were few, kept down the wage of the organized Jewish worker. As for those fields in which Arabs and Jews worked side by side—the railways, post, and telegraph—it was obvious that "no improvement of the working conditions of Jewish workers is possible without the active participation of the Arab worker. *The creation of an organized class of Jewish and Arab workers* is an essential condition if cultured workers are to fill these jobs." Ben-Gurion went still further: "The establishment of *one common front* of all the country's workers, to deal with all their common affairs, is the obligation and right of all pioneers of labor in this country."

Ben-Gurion's resolution read as follows:

> The Histadrut Council instructs the Executive Committee to determine methods for promoting the joint association and cooperation of Jews and Arabs who work in the railways, post and telegraph. The Executive Committee will appoint suitable persons from among its members to handle the affairs of this organization, in coordination with the Union of Hebrew Railway Workers.

The draft resolution was carried, and for the first time, the Histadrut was committed to a clear stand vis-à-vis Arab workers. For although it was true that the text spoke only of railway, postal, and telegraph workers, it bore a more ambitious title: "The Joint Association of Hebrew and Arab Workers." The implication was that cooperation might be extended in the future to other workplaces, such as the port of Haifa, the Nesher cement factory, and the Palestine Electric Company.[4]

But the matter became more complicated during the subsequent congress of the Histadrut's union of railway workers, in February 1922. The resolution passed by the Histadrut Council was at the center of the debate, for the Jewish union was now called on to work for the establishment of an Arab union. Some of the workers advocated the creation of a single union, without regard to race, religion, or nationality; however, the members finally endorsed the resolution of the Histadrut Council.[5] But at the last moment, Ben-Gurion introduced a modification, for he undoubtedly heard from those better informed than he that the prospects for the massive and immediate organization of Arab railway workers were nil. Nine months later, Ben-Gurion would write to the railway union that "on the Arab question, we are in full agreement with you. At this moment, it is still impossible to organize the mass of Arab workers, and so we must find ways to establish ties with selected, individual Arabs."[6] This modification of the Histadrut Council's resolution ran as follows: "Until there are enough Arab workers prepared to form a national union, individual Arab workers will be accepted as members by the union of Jewish workers. Once they grow more numerous, a national union will be formed." The modification passed unanimously. Ben-Gurion was prepared, at least in this instance, to admit Arabs as members of the Histadrut, a policy at odds with the principles of the federation. It was a bold maneuver.

The rest of his moves were made in accordance with the original resolution of the Histadrut Council. As "suitable persons" to handle the joint association railway workers, Ben-Gurion appointed Itzhak Ben-Zvi and himself. The matter was too important to be entrusted to others. It was now in Ben-Gurion's line of duty to meet from time to time with railway workers, both Jews and Arabs, to hear about their problems and the refusal of management to recognize their union. Ben-Gurion would write in his diary of their demand for protection against arbitrary dismissal and their requests for medical assistance, accident insurance, and legal aid.

But Ben-Gurion and Ben-Zvi had little to show for their efforts. In a report submitted in February 1923, they reported that "as of this moment, we have not succeeded in assembling even the nucleus around which a reasonable number of Arab workers might form." There had merely been a few joint workers' meetings to discuss the withholding of severance pay and wage cuts. But Ben-Gurion did not relent and even proposed that the Histadrut Executive appoint a "special secretary," fluent and literate in Arabic, to "keep in constant touch with the Arab worker."[7]

In the meantime, the doors of the Histadrut's railway union were opened to Arab workers on a temporary basis, and the numbers of those interested in joining proved greater than anticipated. Theirs was an interest rooted not in ideological consciousness or commitment to class struggle but in pragmatic considerations. "They think that we have influence in the government, and so wish to join the Histadrut," explained one labor activist.[8] The Histadrut's sick fund also exercised a powerful attraction on the Arab railway workers. A dual process was now underway. On the one hand, Jewish workers were quitting work in the railways, post, and telegraph because of the long hours and low wages. On the other hand, the number of Arab railway workers in the Histadrut union increased, and by 1926 they outnumbered the Jewish workers, 422 to 358. Furthermore, the potential for growth in the Arab membership was much greater, for although the Jewish members constituted 90.3 percent of all Jewish railway workers, Arab members constituted only 21.3 percent of Arab railway workers.[9] This expansion in Arab membership utterly transformed the union.

The demand that the Histadrut cease to be known as a federation of "Hebrew workers" soon surfaced in the railworkers' union, and became more insistent from one year to the next. It was coupled with a demand that the Histadrut function strictly as a labor union and abandon its commitment to Zionist agricultural settlement and industrial development. A faction of extreme leftists championed this call for de-Zionization of the Histadrut, and Ben-Gurion took up the challenge, at a congress of railworkers held in March 1924. There, he heard the request of Arab delegates that the word *Hebrew* be dropped from the Histadrut's name, because it left many Arab workers suspicious of the federation's real aims. One of the Arab participants promised that "if this word is deleted, then we can unite and work together."[10] From the far left, Ben-Gurion heard the demand that the railworkers' union simply secede from the Histadrut: the Histadrut was Zionist, and Zionism meant nothing less than the displacement of the Arab worker.

Ben-Gurion ascended the podium to put forth counterarguments.[11] There were areas of common concern to Jews and Arabs in the field of labor: the right to organize, length of working day, wages, relations with management, accident insurance, and so on. But in other respects, Jews and Arabs had different needs, for one aim of the labor movement was to raise the cultural level of workers who were, in this instance, of two different cultures. For this reason, the Histadrut sought no more than an affiliation with the Arab labor movement. At the same time, Ben-Gurion argued that the railworkers' union had no future outside the Histadrut, for without the support of a large federation, no railway strike could succeed. Neither could an independent railworker's union operate a sick fund or a cooperative. To those who opposed the Histadrut's Zionist vocation, Ben-Gurion argued that the only way to strengthen the labor movement in Palestine was to increase the number of laborers, principally through Jewish immigration. In the end, Ben-Gurion succeeded in checking the drive toward de-Zionization, and the proposal that the railworkers' union secede failed to carry the day. But the contest was far from over.

Ben-Gurion then drew up a proposal designed to take the wind out of the sails of any plan to create a binational labor federation.[12] It essentially postulated a "workers' league," uniting separate Jewish and Arab labor federations, a proposal that represented a further elaboration of Ben-Gurion's earlier ideas on the subject. But now he added a political element. The league would pave the way for a political settlement with the Arabs, circumventing all dialogue with the oppressive effendis who led the Arab national movement. "We have no shared program with the Arab ruling class. But we do share a program with the Arab workers." For the Jewish worker could not work an eight-hour day if the Arab worker could be coerced into laboring ten or twelve hours a day. If the Arab worker settled for fifteen piastres, who then would pay the Jewish worker thirty piastres? For the time being, the league remained a paper proposal, but Ben-Gurion took a number of preliminary steps. The first was the publication of a workers' newspaper in Arabic. *Ittihad al-Amal*—"The Union of Labor"—began to appear in 1926, under the editorial hand of Itzhak Ben-Zvi. At the same time, Arab workers' clubs were founded in Haifa and Jaffa.

Ben-Gurion simultaneously maneuvered the expulsion of the extreme leftists from the railworkers' union, still another triumph. But this success was pregnant with failure, for the struggle between Ben-Gurion and the leftists weakened the trust of the Arabs in the Histadrut and eventually led to their departure from the union *en masse*. The Arab workers gravitated toward the formation of their own federation, but it was not the kind envisioned by Ben-Gurion, for it became an instrument of Muslim religious agitation against the Jews. The railworkers' union, the foundation of Ben-Gurion's joint association, had crumbled to dust. Injections of Histadrut money, and the establishment of loan funds and housing aid for Arab workers, were to no avail. The union floundered, and in 1929, Arab railway workers founded their own union, putting an end to the most ambitious of the cooperative ventures.

The political conception of the Arab issue that held sway among the leaders of Ahdut Ha'avodah—Ben-Gurion, Katznelson, and Tabenkin—derived from the declared aim of the Balfour Declaration: establishment of a National Home in Palestine on both banks of the Jordan, with the help of Great Britain, without infringing on Arab rights. From the outset, they envisioned the separate development of Jews and Arabs as desirable if not essential to the success of the National Home policy. And the active role would be reserved for the Jews, as Ben-Gurion explained: "The assets of the Jewish National Home must be created exclusively through our own work, for only the product of Hebrew labor can serve as the national estate."[13] The Arab role would be the passive one of continuing to live as they always had and staying out from under foot so as not to get hurt. Since the founders of Ahdut Ha'avodah anticipated a Jewish state, the Arab rights they sought to preserve were civil rather than political, and could best be protected through the absolute segregation of the country's inhabitants into two national communities.

The principle of separation had already compromised the notion of class solidarity in the doctrinal formulations of Ben-Gurion. Once the British mandatory authorities began to float plans for a legislative council, an embryonic parliament of Palestine, the prospect of democratic rule by the majority—an Arab majority—posed still another ideological challenge. The matter became the subject of controversy between Ben-Gurion and Shlomo Kaplansky during the Ahdut Ha'avodah conference held in Ein Harod in May 1924. Kaplansky was one of the founders of Poalei Zion, and he stood squarely to the left of Ben-Gurion.

Kaplansky not only favored a legislative council, but demanded that the British give it the widest possible authority. "Let us not be stingy in the matter of the parliament's authority. We should come to an agreement with the Arabs, and together demand the expansion of the parliament's jurisdiction and ultimate self-rule." To defend the rights of the Jewish minority, Kaplansky proposed the creation of two houses: a house of representatives elected "democratically," which would, of course, have an Arab majority "for the time being," and a senate in which Jews and Arabs would have equal representation.

Kaplansky simultaneously argued for a political initiative that would open a dialogue with the Arabs. He lamented the lack of any sustained contact between the Zionist organization and the Arabs; such negotiations as were necessary were invariably conducted through the British, an intolerable situation. For the Near East was being swept by a great movement of liberation, and the farsighted action would be to strike a bargain with the Arabs, even if this meant treating with the effendis. Of course, dealing with this reactionary leadership was difficult and distasteful, but each national movement originated in a ruling class, which was the first to drape itself in the flag of freedom and exploit mass idealism. Such were the beginnings of every movement of national liberation; and the fellah would play no role in the parliament at first. But in the meantime, we should approach the Arab masses, meet with them, and expose the effendis for what they are, even as we sit with them in parliament.[14]

Ben-Gurion then unfolded his critique of Kaplansky's "error." The effendis, he stressed, were not genuinely interested in parliamentary or democratic rule; they wanted the power to dominate, to make themselves masters of the country, and to decide the fate of the Zionist endeavor. We should not fear to declare openly that there can be no common language between Jewish workers and the effendis who now control the Arab movement. That was a reality that could not be disregarded; disheartening as it may be, no agreement was possible. The shortcut of a settlement with the Arabs through the effendis was not Ahdut Ha'avodah's way.

Instead bridges had to be built to the Arab worker who, though still a politically negligible force, would one day emerge triumphant. It was, in fact, the historic mission of Zionism to elevate the Arab worker, without whom it would be difficult for Labor Zionism to succeed, for the fate of the Jewish worker was bound up with that of his Arab comrade. Ben-Gurion finally presented his alternative plan, based on national autonomy for Jews and Arabs, in which the mandatory government would continue to play a decisive role.[15]

The differences between Kaplansky and Ben-Gurion were fundamental. Kaplansky favored Jewish–Arab cooperation now, in a parliament and government that would exercise authority over the entire country without the aid of Great Britain. Ben-Gurion preferred that separation of the two peoples be maintained and that each enjoy a measure of autonomy under British supervision. Cooperation would come only later, when the Arab worker was prepared for it.

The two men also differed over settlement policy. Kaplansky urged that Jews should settle throughout the country, but Ben-Gurion favored settlement in concentrations, wherein the Jews could enjoy the fullest possible autonomy. One participant in the conference later saw in retrospect that Ben-Gurion was laying the foundations of a Jewish state, while Kaplansky seemed to lean toward a binational state.

Katznelson sided with Ben-Gurion. Did parliamentary democracy in the Palestinian context not mean putting the minority in the hands of the majority? Could we agree that tomorrow the majority be allowed to legislate on economic, legal, civil, and labor matters? Could we hand over our lives, our language, our schools, and our families to the majority? Would this not constitute, in the most humanitarian sense, the grossest miscarriage of justice? Formal democracy, Katznelson argued, was undesirable, because it meant forfeiting our fates to the whims of others. For it was clear that such a parliament would impede Jewish immigration and settlement.[16]

Tabenkin also took up Ben-Gurion's cause, but with socialist arguments. To hand authority over to the effendis was to block the country's progress. The present Arab majority, in fact, utilized only a small portion of the land and had no right to stand in the way of development. On the lips of the feudal effendis, the word democracy had nothing to do with the liberation of the oppressed. In effect, the demand was reactionary, for it meant handing the country over to those who had no interest in its economic development and every intention of exploiting the populace.[17]

The debate over Kaplansky's proposal exposed the inconsistencies in the Labor Zionist program of Ahdut Ha'avodah. The principles of democratic rule by majority and the equality of all nations were compromised by Ahdut Ha'avodah's insistence on the right of Jews to immigrate, to settle, to form a majority, and to eventually establish a Jewish state. National solidarity dislodged class solidarity in this order of priorities. The movement's leaders were led by their logic to reject parliamentary democracy and to favor the continued rule of an imperialist power. They demanded discrimination in the workplace in favor of the Jewish worker, in glaring opposition to the principle of solidarity among all workers. But for Ben-Gurion, Katznelson, and Tabenkin, there were always extenuating circumstances that tempered absolute principles. The role of leadership played by the effendis among the Arabs justified the rejection of democracy; the need to rebuild the Jew justified discrimination against Arab labor. Ben-Gurion

never put his arguments in the blunt terms once used by David Remez, when asked in 1925 about the "Arab problem": "Listen, is it because you've already solved the Jewish problem that you pester me with the Arabs?"[18] Ben-Gurion preferred circuitous formulations: "I am unwilling to forego even one percent of Zionism for 'peace'—yet I do not want Zionism to infringe upon even one percent of legitimate Arab rights."[19] But if Jews and Arabs were unprepared to forgo any of their rights, they obviously could not live side by side without doing injustice to one another. And if Ahdut Ha'avodah was unprepared to make any concessions, its doctrine would be riddled with inconsistencies.

Ben-Gurion presented the alternative of autonomy.[20] National autonomy in Palestine, as a first step toward a Jewish state, had been acceptable to Zionists and Labor Zionists almost from the beginning of the Zionist enterprise. As early as 1906, Ben-Gurion envisioned the agricultural settlements—the "Hebrew republics" as he called them—as the seed of future autonomy. The National Home policy, sanctioned by the Balfour Declaration, was interpreted by Ben-Gurion as a British commitment to the creation of a Jewish state through national autonomy. The form this autonomy was to take would be territorial and personal: areas of concentrated Jewish settlement would enjoy territorial autonomy, and Jews scattered throughout predominantly Arab areas would enjoy the protection of personal autonomy.

What of the Arabs? Were they, too, worthy of autonomy? In 1918, Ben-Gurion called for "full internal autonomy in all cultural, economic, and social affairs" for them as well. The idea of two separate autonomes, Jewish and Arab, was endorsed by both Poalei Zion and Ahdut Ha'avodah. This principle of separation created the ideological climate in which the Arabs came to be known as "neighbors" and relations with the Arabs as "relations among neighbors." When, in 1931, Ben Gurion published a collection of his speeches and articles on Arab issues, he gave the book the revealing title *We and Our Neighbors*. The usage reflected his concept of the absolute separation of inhabitants of the same country according to national affiliation.

Although Ben-Gurion did not provide any particulars, it was obvious that as "our neighbors" the Arabs would enjoy a form of autonomy somewhat different from Jewish autonomy. For the Jewish autonome was ultimately destined to evolve into a Jewish state and disappear, whereas the Arabs would never have more than their autonomy. This inequality was written into the Balfour Declaration and the provisions of the League of Nations Mandate, which committed the power that administered the country to favor the establishment of the Jewish National Home.

Ben-Gurion was well aware that the Arabs opposed the prospect of a Jewish majority and the very idea of a National Home. They demanded an independent Arab Palestine. On their account, the British administration, first military and then civil, recoiled from the policy embodied in the Balfour Declaration and the League of Nations Mandate. Because Ben-Gurion recognized the depth of this Arab opposition, as expressed during the violence of 1920 and 1921, he began to speak more often of the need to avoid any infringement of the "civil and religious" rights of the non-Jewish communities. The Balfour Declaration also required such caution, and the concept became a fundamental premise of Ben-Gurion's doctrine.

But beyond this, Ben-Gurion's remarks on just what kind of autonomy the Arabs would enjoy remained clouded in ambiguity. Not so, of course, his opinions on Jewish autonomy, which were highly developed and refined. The Jews were to have their own parliament, and a national committee, which would elect a government. In Ben-Gurion's scheme, the British authorities would cede wide spheres of jurisdiction to these Jewish representative bodies, which would virtually govern towns and settlements inhabited by Jews. Blocs of Jewish population would be linked by belts of Jewish settlement, creating large regions in which the right of Jewish autonomous government would run unimpeded. Ben-Gurion opposed the proposal that Jews enjoy autonomy in a narrowly personal sense, or that their obligations to the autonome be voluntary. The representative institutions would have binding authority within their territorial jurisdictions over all Jews. These bodies would be entrusted with extensive powers, including taxation. The tasks of the British administration would be reduced to the preservation of public security and the maintenance of the country's economic infrastructure. Police, criminal justice, ports, posts, telegraph, railways, and public health would fall within the British sphere. "All other governmental tasks must be handed over to the self-governing institutions, to the autonome and the municipalities." This emphasis on full autonomy over territory, combined with Ben-Gurion's aim of concentrated Jewish settlement, pointed in the direction of a virtual partition of the country into Jewish and Arab regions. In future, Ben-Gurion would even propose that the Jewish quarters of cities secede and establish their own separate municipalities.

There was the question of what would become of Jews in predominantly Arab areas, but here, Ben-Gurion allowed the principle of personal autonomy. To make his point, he emphasized the cultural gap that, in his perception, divided the two peoples. It would not be fair to supply the identical type of services—here he cited education—to Jews of advanced culture and Arabs of backward culture. Jews would suffer if laws suitable to a wider, generally illiterate population were imposed upon them. Only wide autonomy for all Jews could defend this progressive minority and enable it to develop and grow.

As to what the Arabs would make of their own autonomous status, Ben-Gurion had nothing to say. As early as 1919, he differed with Kaplansky on this point. Ben-Gurion never went further than to say that the Arabs, too, had the right to autonomy; he never attempted to define its character or extent. Even this recognition came from his pen only in the mid-1920s; before that, it can only be inferred from the manifestos he wrote for Ahdut Ha'avodah. But Kaplansky, as early as 1919, determined that "both peoples in this country, Jews and Arabs, are guaranteed national autonomy on a personal basis, and will enjoy national equity of rights in municipalities and local governments." Kaplansky even detailed the scope of Arab autonomy, specifying that it would include administration of Muslim religious endowments (*awqaf*). He was already moving in the direction of support for a binational state, with his stand in favor of personal autonomy, and he also promised that "the national languages of the Jews and Arabs will enjoy equal status."[21] But all that Ben-Gurion would say was that "we have no intention of dominating others. When we speak of a state, we mean two things: that others not dominate us, and that we not live in anarchy. We want to govern ourselves."[22] The furthest he ventured from nondomination was in a formulation dating from 1925. Again, he did not offer any detailed statement about the extent of Arab autonomy. But he relied on the adage of the sages not to do unto others what is hateful unto oneself. "What we demand for ourselves, we demand for others, and what we wish others to give us, we ourselves are prepared to give, *for better or for worse*."[23] This was Ben-Gurion's promise for the day when the Jews would constitute a majority.

In 1925, Ahdut Ha'avodah endorsed Ben-Gurion's plan for territorial autonomy, after much controversy and debate. But the plan finally approved by the British administration in 1928 fell far short of that envisioned by Ben-Gurion. The legal personality of the Jewish "community" was officially recognized, but the basis of that personality was religious. This meant that membership in the community was a matter of personal conscience and any Jew could opt out. The only authority that the representative Jewish institutions exercised was that conferred by voluntary, personal consent. And such autonomy as the "community" enjoyed applied to persons and not territory. For this reason, its effective scope was less than that envisioned by Ben-Gurion. Virtually all of the community's activities—the leveling of taxes, elections to a representative body, appointment of a rabbinical council—were subject to the approval and inspection of the British administration. But Ben-Gurion was farsighted enough to envision the eventual transformation of this personal autonomy into territorial autonomy and the evolution of *Knesset Israel*, the organized Jewish community, into the self-governing Jewish state.

6

"This Is a National Movement"

It was Ben-Gurion's claim that no contradiction existed between the aspirations of Labor Zionism and those of the country's Arab inhabitants. His interpretation of Zionism as a just movement, and his plan for the virtual segregation of Jews and Arabs in Palestine, combined in a pastoral vision of neighbors living separately but in harmony. For Ben-Gurion, a solution to the "Arab question," if such a question did exist, was within easy grasp. He stood by that conviction throughout the controversy surrounding Jewish and Arab rights at the Western (or Wailing) Wall, a dispute that ended in violence and brought seven years of tranquility to a shuddering halt.

The dispute over the Western Wall arose, on the one hand, from the Arab fear that Jewish worshipers wished to establish a claim to the site and, on the other, from the Jewish fear that Muslim authorities sought to prevent access to the holy place, since the property constituted part of a Muslim religious endowment. The policy of the British administration rested on the status quo ante of Ottoman times, by which Jews were permitted access to the Wall strictly for purposes of prayer. No benches or partitions between male and female worshipers could be set up on the narrow premises. Neither could Jews pray vociferously as a congregation or sound the shofar. Ultimately, the Jewish worshipers failed to abide by these restrictions, exciting the apprehensions of Muslims keen to defend their own holy sites just above the Wall, where stand the Dome of the Rock and the Aqsa Mosque.

To those who championed the Jewish right to full worship at the Wall, among them Jabotinsky, Ben-Gurion warned against a trap that he thought had been set by the British administration to draw the Jews into a "bloody war of religion." Ben-Gurion pleaded that "we not give our oppressors an opportunity to spread the libel that Jewish settlement constitutes a threat to Muslim and Christian holy places."[1] The conflict escalated, but a cautious Zionist policy took shape, characterized by sharp protests to the mandatory government and self-restraint in the vicinity of the Wall to avoid anything that might be interpreted by Arabs as a provocation. The rationale for this policy was the apprehension that the Mufti of Jerusalem, Haj Amin al-Husseini, would seek to exploit the Western Wall dispute in order to provoke disturbances, and would enjoy the tacit support of certain British officials. While the Arabs became more and more violent in their confrontations with Jewish worshipers, the leaders of the Yishuv called for restraint. These appeals were reiterated in August 1929 with the approach of the Ninth of Av, the anniversary of the destruction of the Temple of which the Wall is the last remnant.

But the Revisionists took a different approach, and organized a demonstration for the Ninth of Av. In violation of their permit, the demonstrators turned their march to the Wall into a nationalist manifestation, with flags, speeches, and the singing of the national anthem, *Hatikvah*. This gave Amin al-Husseini the pretext needed to organize a counterdemonstration the following day. These events started the country down the slippery slope leading to riots in Jerusalem a week later. The violence soon spread throughout the country, especially afflicting Hebron, Motza, Tel Aviv, Jaffa, Haifa, the Jezreel Valley, the Galilee, and Safed. Before it was over, in a week's time, 133 Jews were dead and 339 injured.

At that moment, Ben-Gurion was abroad. Two days after the first outbreak, the news caught up with him in Genoa. The account that he found in the pages of a local newspaper stunned him. In his diary, he wrote that "things have gone too far. The Western Wall dispute has turned Jerusalem into a field of slaughter, just as I thought it would."[2] The reports he found later in the day in the London *Times* and *Observer* brought still worse news. "The disaster is greater than I thought," he added in his diary.[3] His first reaction came in a cable that he sent to the Zionist Executive in London, from the ship that bore him straightaway to Palestine. Essentially he reiterated the charges he had leveled in 1920 and 1921 against officials in the mandatory government. The cable demanded the "removal of the officials responsible for the disaster, severe sentences for the guilty, and full compensation for all damages."[4]

He continued to pursue this line of attack even after his return. "It's up to us to see that the officials don't get off scot free," he declared, and then went still further: "Responsibility for the panic in the country rests entirely upon the chiefs of the administration." Ben-Gurion did note that a number of officials had acquitted their difficult tasks honorably, and he exempted the high commissioner from the indictment since he, too, had been abroad at the fateful hour. But the others stood accused of criminal negligence: "The high officials did not intervene against the open agitation, took no measures to prevent massacres and destruction, equated the rioters with defenders, and encouraged the rioters and murderers through their inaction." He did not go as far as some of his colleagues, who claimed that the British administration actually initiated the violence. But his accusations were serious nonetheless.[5]

Yet far more than in 1920 and 1921, Ben-Gurion's responses inclined toward the exploitation of the catastrophe in order to advance the Zionist enterprise. When the full magnitude of the events became apparent to him, he launched an appeal for the recruitment of 50,000 young immigrants. "The mood in the Jewish world must be exploited in order to mobilize the maximal effort for settlement."[6] And he would exploit the pride of the Jewish people in the heroism shown by the few against the many, to fortify the Yishuv from within. Ben-Gurion blatantly used the events to close the ranks of world Jewry around the issue of Palestine. "Not only the 160,000" Jews of Palestine, but "the sixteen million worldwide, will defend their historic inheritance." The first step was the bringing of more capital and more people to the country, through the dispatch of special emissaries to Europe and America. The funds thus collected would not go to aid the affected families or even to reconstruction. Such compensation was the responsibility of the mandatory government. The considerable funds amassed in the wake of the violence would be devoted "only to new building, to new foundations and expansion." The ambitious plan was to collect 5 million pounds and bring in 50,000 young immigrants within a year; with the money, it would be possible to settle 10,000 newcomers at 2000 sites.[7]

The final product of this plan would be a marked improvement in the security of the Yishuv. The 50,000 youths would go far to balance the forces in Palestine, for once a balance was struck, "then we need not fear the Arabs." How was it that the addition of 50,000 Jews to the existing Yishuv of 160,000 could even the scales against 800,000 Arabs? Ben-Gurion held that a single Jewish fighter, thanks to his education, higher cultural level, and superior motivation, was the equal of several Arabs. Although he never specified the precise ratio, Ben-Gurion thus set down the principle of relative quality, which alone would enable the few to stand up to the many. At the same time, he urged that the new points of settlement be established between existing settlements, in order to secure a measure of territorial contiguity. In one manifesto,[8] Ben-Gurion wrote of an "iron wall of workers' settlements surrounding every Hebrew city and town, land and human bridges that would link isolated points." Here was also an opportunity to enforce the principle of exclusive employment of Hebrew labor by Jews—*Avodah Ivrit*. During the week of bloodshed, Arab workers had failed to show for work in Jewish-owned citrus groves, and the farmers had no alternative but to hire Hebrew labor. Ben-Gurion's aim was to perpetuate this situation, and from the outset he spoke of the need to exploit the violence on behalf of *Avodah Ivrit*. "Our main problem is to translate the people's shock into action for fortifying the Yishuv," he told the Histadrut Council, and he declared himself for the principle of "100% Hebrew labor." The aim of all this activity was twofold: to ensure the growth of the Yishuv and to set it apart as an essentially autonomous entity. Such was Ben-Gurion's reaction in September 1929, under the immediate impact of events. His every move was dictated by his commitment to his plan for autonomy.

In Ben-Gurion's view, the Yishuv, simultaneously growing and withdrawing within itself, had to strive all the same toward friendly relations with its Arab neighbors. He was severely critical of the Revisionist approach, which was liable to intensify conflict with the Arabs and ultimately foil Zionism. Ben-Gurion did everything within his power to discredit Jabotinsky's doctrine and its expositors in Palestine.

> Now more than ever, we must stand guard lest we fall into a chauvinistic mood. Like a putrid weed thriving on foul water, the Revisionist pestilence is liable to spread now in the Yishuv. Hooligans of the written and spoken word who formerly made their livings through incitements and accusations against the workers have now turned to others, and

> in empty-headed and sickening noisiness, with deceitful and foolish trumpet-calls of victory, they inflame the passions of the enemy, and defile our pure and profound grief. We must rise against this perverted national fanaticism, and against the worthless prattle of sham heroes, whose lips becloud the moral purity of our national movement and distort the redemptive and humanitarian content of the Zionist idea.

Ben-Gurion's alternative was to fully uphold Jewish claims and rights, while showing "careful, meticulous and wise consideration for the rights and feelings of others."[9]

Ben-Gurion's initial reaction of laying blame for the violence at the doorstep of the administration was essentially a play for time. The magnitude of the 1929 riots, which culminated in massacres in Hebron, Motza, and Safed, demanded that he clarify his stand on the "Arab question," and he needed time to gather his thoughts. Were these once again the machinations of the effendis and the deeds of criminals—the "human scum" of 1920? Or were the riots the work of a national movement, seeking in its own fashion to assert its identity in the pursuit of freedom and independence? Had the acts been inspired by effendis and clerics anxious to preserve their feudal rule, or were they expressions of a national movement fearful that the Zionists would dispossess Palestinian Arabs of their lands through immigration and settlement?

Ben-Gurion had come face to face with the contradictions inherent in his professed position that no national contradiction existed between Jews and Arabs. In truth, he had already admitted the existence of an Arab national movement, and had called it by name. In July 1922, after an Arab commercial strike organized by the Muslim Executive Council, Ben-Gurion wrote in his diary: "The success of the Arabs in organizing the closure of shops shows that we are dealing here with a national movement. For the Arabs, this is an important educational step."[10] In December of the same year he declared that "a national war is being waged against us."[11]

He must have been alert to the contradiction between this assessment and his distinction in September 1929 between good Arabs and bad Arabs. But there was even an occasion on which he contradicted himself in the same party statement:

> The attack of the Yishuv which was prepared and organized by the Mufti of Jerusalem was not only the work of the gang of effendis who control the Supreme Muslim Council and the Muslim-Christian Committee. It was the urban and rural *masses* who participated in the attacks, especially the Beduin. The lust for theft and murder overwhelmed a large segment of the Arab population in the country. Any belittling of the peril which threatened the Yishuv and which still hangs over it, is a dangerous and damaging illusion. We stood before an outbreak of the worst instincts of the wild mob: fearful religious fanaticism, lust for theft and pillage, the thirst for blood. And the aim was clear and terrible: the destruction of the Yishuv.[12]

How could this be reconciled with what followed? It was a

> . . . fact that many Arab villages, and most of the Arab villages near our farms, did not participate in this attack. The great majority of Arab villagers did not lend a hand to the murderers and robbers, despite the insidious propaganda and incitements by instigators sent to urge the Arab villagers to attack their Jewish neighbors.

Who, then, were the Arabs of Palestine—the masses inflamed by religious fanaticism, bent on destroying the Yishuv, or the great majority of villagers who were unmoved by the agitation? To whom did the national movement belong, to the former or the latter?

At least three explanations to the contradictions in Ben-Gurion's statement suggest themselves. First, Arab spokesmen—the Arab Executive Committee, the Supreme Muslim Council, the newspapers, and so on—initially disassociated themselves from the violence, arguing that it did not serve the Arab cause. Only later did they arrive at a completely different stance, according to which those Arabs who were executed for perpetrating the massacre in Hebron were innocent "martyrs . . . and the pathfinders of freedom and independence." Second, the Arab national movement took time to define its public position toward the events; Ben-Gurion still may have held the view that denying the national conflict between Jews and Arabs could help to cool tempers. Third, the contradictions may have evidenced internal party differences of opinion. In his statements on behalf of his party colleagues, Ben-Gurion had to make room for the many and contradictory opinions that flourished within Ahdut Ha'avodah and Hapoel Hatzair.

But because Ben-Gurion never signed a party document without agreeing with everything it contained, perhaps he was simply undecided. This groping for a coherent explanation for the violence surfaced in a consultation to which he summoned party activists in regular contact with Arab workers and peasants.[13] The aim of the gathering, which met in November 1929, was to clarify "the possibilities for action to establish peaceful relations between ourselves and our neighbors, first of all in the villages." At the outset, he expressed agreement with those who interpreted the disturbances as a "holy war." In speaking of the religious agitation launched by the Mufti of Jerusalem, Ben-Gurion maintained that "national incitement would not have succeeded in moving the masses, but the religious incitement which issued from sources trusted by the peasants, laid the groundwork for the riots." Nor did Ben-Gurion forget to mention the attractions of looting as an Arab motive.

But in the same breath, he criticized those who denied the existence of an Arab national movement and its role in the violence. These doubters were quick to cite clan rivalries, and the differences that divided the Mufti from his opponents, the Muslims from the Christians, and the fellahs from the

Bedouin, in order to claim that without "positive content," there could be no Arab national movement. In response, Ben-Gurion had this to say:

> It is true that the Arab national movement has no positive content. The leaders of the movement are unconcerned with the betterment of the people and provision of their essential needs. They do not aid the fellah; to the contrary, the leaders suck his blood, and exploit the popular awakening for private gain. But we err if we measure the Arabs and their movement by our standards. Every people is worthy of its national movement. The obvious characteristic of a political movement is that it knows how to mobilize the masses. From this perspective there is no doubt that we are facing a political movement, and we should not underestimate it.
>
> A national movement mobilizes masses, and that is the main thing. The Arab movement is not one of revival, and its moral value is dubious. But in a political sense, this is a national movement.

This was a landmark in the evolution of Ben-Gurion's appreciation of the Arabs. In 1916, he wrote in his Omaha notes that "the Arabs are not organized as a nation. They do not have one national party but many parties." But now Ben-Gurion was prepared to change the yardstick by which he measured political reality. In 1916, that yardstick had been the advanced national movements, similar to the full-fledged liberation movements of today: by 1929, it was the simple organizational ability to mobilize the masses.

Then why did Ben-Gurion persist in labeling the disturbances a "holy war" even behind closed doors and in intimate company, and to describe them as the result of religious agitation? Why did he maintain that "national incitement would not have succeeded in moving the masses"? Why did he not employ his new yardstick, measure the ability of the Arab national movement to mobilize the masses, and then declare unequivocally that the religious appeal was part and parcel of Palestinian Arab national sentiment—that this was a national movement with a unique religious dimension?

The implications of such a declaration would have been profound and divisive. At that very moment, the Zionist parties were demanding that the mandatory administration not "reward the rioters." They insisted on trials and severe sentences for all who incited and took part in the violence. Since there was no doubt that the Arab national movement bore responsibility, how could it now be rewarded with Zionist recognition? On this issue, Ben-Gurion had no desire to break Zionist ranks. Would such recognition not signify that the Palestinian Arabs constituted a distinct people, and were not simply one branch of a great Arab people?

Such an admission might have far-reaching implications. The existence of this people would raise profound doubts about Labor Zionism as a just movement. As part of a great Arab people, the Arabs of Palestine could be granted civil rights in a Jewish state and regard the independence of neighboring Arab states as their own political fulfillment. But if there existed a separate Palestinian Arab people, was it not entitled to self-determination in its own country, Palestine? As a just movement, Labor Zionism would have to appeal for the equal division of both civil and *political* rights between Jews and Arabs. That pointed to possible partition.

What finally drove Ben-Gurion to cut through the contradictions were two fears. The first was of the Yishuv's possible destruction by Arabs from Palestine and neighboring countries, "for instance in an outbreak by Arab tribes from beyond Palestine against the Jews within Palestine." The second was the fear that renewed Arab attacks, even if they were successfully repulsed by the Haganah, would convince wary Jews to steer clear of Palestine. Insecurity, he wrote to the Zionist Executive, was liable to diminish the "attractiveness" of Palestine for the Jewish people and discourage immigration. "The feeling that Jews are sitting on a volcano could undermine the whole Zionist movement. Jews will see the country not as a haven but as a battlefield."[14] Even after the suppression of the disorders by British military muscle, Ben-Gurion emphasized that the process had only begun. "The political violence is just beginning."[15] His conclusion was that "for our enterprise and the Zionist movement, we must *prevent the danger* of attack, and must *create a feeling* of *security*. Without that feeling, there can be no building for the generations ahead, and no consistent flow of new capital and people."[16] The fortification of the Yishuv was one response. Political effort was the other. Ben-Gurion had reached the conclusion that force alone would not suffice.

7
Not by Force Alone

Ben-Gurion admitted that the violence of 1929 led both him and the Yishuv to define "the political question of our relations with the Arabs" and to propose an answer.[1] His early inclination to exploit the disturbances yielded to apprehension that the Arabs might prove capable of upsetting Zionist plans with renewed outbreaks. "The flow of pioneering immigration will not be diverted by the danger," he wrote in a memorandum to the Zionist Executive. "But the plain Jew, practical and pragmatic, will ask whether he should abandon his property, life, and family, to a country ripe for pogroms."[2]

The political aftermath worried Ben-Gurion still more: "The influence of the violence is perhaps more damaging and dangerous than the things which actually happened during those awful days."[3] The Shaw Commission was now investigating the causes of the bloodshed, "and logic dictates a change in England's policy."[4] In short, "if we do not learn the lesson of these events, we will truly be without hope, and we shall be cheating our future."[5]

Ben-Gurion's answer was a federation. He first made explicit mention of the concept in a memorandum to the Socialist International concerning the disturbances in Palestine.[6] It was, of course, necessary to employ Marxist catchwords and jargon in writing for this audience, and to lay the blame at the feet of the reactionary front of capitalists, landowners, and clerics. Here he stuck to a conventional interpretation. The violence was the work of "vandals," "mobs incited and inflamed by the fire of religious fanaticism," and "the rabble bent upon pillage."

This was not a national protest against the Mandate and the Jewish National Home. In fact, Zionism brought nothing but progress to the Arabs, and especially to the Arab workers. "The outbreak of destruction and bloodshed was not the result of bad relations or continuous disputes between Jews and Arabs." It was, first of all, the result of incitement by the effendis, who feared the effects of the Jewish example on the exploited Arabs. "Class fear is one of the principal factors in the hostile incitement against the Yishuv launched by the effendis."

In making these charges, Ben-Gurion was pandering to the socialist prejudices of his audience. He, himself, knew better, as he had shown in his simultaneous discussions on Arab nationalism with party activists. The exit from this impasse, Ben-Gurion located for the Socialist International in the establishment of two separate autonomes. These would learn to live side by side, and "then a federation can be founded between the two peoples, not on the basis of lust for power by the exploiting classes, but on the principle of self-rule in internal affairs and shared control of the country." The idea of a federation was launched. What it now required was articulate exposition.

The impetus came unexpectedly, when Ben-Gurion learned of a plan floated by the eccentric British adviser to King Ibn Saud, H. St. John Philby, in collaboration with Hebrew University Chancellor Judah Leon Magnes. Magnes was an American-born Jew and cultural nationalist, who was prepared to reach a settlement with the Arabs that fell short of Jewish statehood. Despite his objections to the narrowly cultural nationalism, Ben-Gurion had a deep respect for Magnes dating back to Ben-Gurion's arrival in Palestine. In April 1929, Ben-Gurion and Katznelson held a long talk with Magnes, and Ben-Gurion noted in his diary that "from the discussion, it became clear that we did wrong by neglecting this man."[7] The persistence and courage of Magnes made a profound impression on Ben-Gurion. As early as 1921, Magnes had opposed the Balfour Declaration, arguing that it would stir up the Arabs, leading Britain to renege on promises to the Zionists. Since that time, he had maintained that Zionists should settle for freedom of immigration, settlement, and cultural development, but should forget about the idea of a Jewish majority and state. This was the position that Magnes had taken in a major article that Ben-Gurion read, and although Ben-Gurion shared none of the piece's premises, he allowed that "the article is written forcefully and with profound understanding."[8] Ben-Gurion and Magnes had become mutual admirers.

The details of Philby's plan, as Ben-Gurion heard them, were that a parliament and government would be democratically elected in Palestine and would doubtless have Arab majorities. But the mandate would continue in force, and the British high commissioner would have the right to veto all legislation passed by the parliament and government. It would be the high commissioner's task to guarantee the rights of Jews and other minorities, and he would be assisted by the army, which would serve under his command. Jews and Arabs would enjoy the right of free immigration, limited only by the country's economic absorptive capacity. The Jewish Agency would continue to defend Jewish interests. Finally, although the Jews would be free to settle anywhere, they had to abandon forever any idea of establishing a Jewish state. This was essentially a prescription for an Arab Palestine, in which Jews would enjoy protected status.*[9]

"We did not come here to add one more exile—a demeaning and miserable one at that—to our many other exiles." This was Ben-Gurion's unequivocal response. He would not abandon his aspiration for a Jewish majority and a Jewish state. But the plan left him sleepless, and the night after he heard of Philby's scheme, he entered in his diary a counterplan for the government of Palestine, "in accordance with the mandate, the needs of the National Home, and the concerns of the Arabs."[10] The last impediment to the full articulation of his plan for federation was lifted, now that the "political danger" of Philby's negotiations pressed on him.

Ben-Gurion's idea was that separate Jewish and Arab autonomes would be established, which would cooperate with Great Britain in the administration of the mandate. Each autonome would evolve into a canton, "with *full* self-rule" in national, cultural, and religious affairs, and government by a cantonal parliament. The two cantons would then be joined in a federation, under a British high commissioner and a federal government. The high commissioner would be responsible for security and foreign affairs, and would command the police and army. The federal government would be composed of nine cabinet ministers: three Britons elected by the cantonal parliaments from a list prepared by the Colonial Office; three Jews; and three Arabs. The Jews and Arabs would be appointed by the high commissioner from lists submitted to him by each of the cantonal parliaments. The British ministers would hold the portfolios of Justice, the Treasury, and Transportation and Communications. The

* Philby is better known for two later peace plans that he put forth in 1937 and in 1939. But Ben-Gurion did not take those later plans seriously. Philby's biographer, Elizabeth Monroe, in her *Philby of Arabia*, also discounted Philby's later plans as "abortive."

Jewish cabinet members would administer Immigration, Settlement, and Public Works. The three Arab ministers would control Education, Health, and Industry and Commerce. Each cabinet minister would have two assistants, one Jewish and the other Arab.

Noticeable for its absence was all mention of a federal parliament. "The idea of a parliament with fifty-fifty representation is a bad one," explained Ben-Gurion. "Such a parliament would become a wrestling arena." The other notable feature of the plan was the absolute freedom of immigration and settlement to be guaranteed the Jews within their canton. The federation plan remained pressed between the pages of his diary, and he did not yet reveal it to anyone. He would first turn it over in his mind and make numerous refinements and amendments.

But time was growing short. Ben-Gurion was anxious to learn just how far Philby's talks with Magnes had gone, and whether the high commissioner had gotten wind of the proceedings. Ben-Gurion went to Jerusalem to seek out Magnes himself, who told him that although Philby had been in touch with the Arab Executive, he had not made his plan known to the mandatory authorities. Ben-Gurion was relieved. He assured Magnes that the Histadrut, too, desired peace and an agreement with the Arabs, "but in practical politics there may be differences between us, and we ask that from now on, you take no step until we have had the chance to clarify the issue in a thorough manner." Magnes, who wished to publish the proposals raised in his dialogue with Philby, agreed to delay such a move for a day, and consented to meet with Ben-Gurion in Tel Aviv before making any further move.[11]

Ben-Gurion showed marked restraint in addressing Magnes. When someone active alongside Magnes asked Ben-Gurion for his opinion of the Philby talks, Ben-Gurion practically exploded: "You and Magnes don't understand the matter. You are like sleepwalkers who plod about with knife in hand

and slaughter children while unconscious. You are undermining the very spirit of our movement. You must quit this work, because you haven't any political acumen."[12] To Harry Sacher, chairman of the Jewish Agency, Ben-Gurion said: "I see a great political peril in these negotiations, because the high commissioner has already been influenced . . . we have to uproot the evil at its source."[13]

When Magnes arrived in Tel Aviv for his meeting with Ben-Gurion, the latter was disturbed to learn that the high commissioner had reported the content of the Philby proposals to the Colonial Office. If Philby had not revealed the details, then Magnes must have done so in a talk with the high commissioner. But Ben-Gurion remained calm and collected. He and Katznelson, who was also present, attempted to convince Magnes that the Philby plan meant the creation of an Arab state in which Jewish cultural life would stagnate. Not only political Zionism would suffer; so, too, would the progressive causes of workers and women. It would be an effendi state, in which Jews would exist on sufferance. Then Ben-Gurion struck his *coup*: the federation plan he had confided to his diary.[14]

This was a desperate move, prompted by apprehension that events were slipping rapidly out of hand. Ben-Gurion even invited Magnes to his home the next day, to hear him explain the new plan to Ahdut Ha'avodah and Hapoel Hatzair. In a two-and-a-half hour lecture on a Sabbath morning, Ben-Gurion spelled out the details to his party colleagues and Magnes.[15] On the basis of the federation plan, Ben-Gurion pronounced himself ready to deal with the effendis who led the Arab nationalist movement, a complete *volte-face* from the position he had maintained five years earlier in his momentous debate with Shlomo Kaplansky.

Magnes was deeply impressed; Ben-Gurion's party colleagues were more reserved, having been led to believe all along that such a dialogue was unthinkable. But Ben-Gurion was not deterred by these critical responses. He had taken his first step toward a fundamental revision of his approach to the triangular relationship between Britain, the Jews, and the Arabs in Palestine.

Why had Ben-Gurion set aside the idea of Jewish sovereignty in all of Palestine? He was clearly troubled by the failure of Labor Zionism to provide an answer to the question of Arab self-determination. The ideology was grounded in the principles of justice, equality, and freedom, and was consistent with these values. Ben-Gurion held that the fulfillment of Zionism would not come at the expense of Arab rights. But if the Arabs were to be denied self-determination, if they were never to be allowed national expression in the land of their birth, how could Zionism genuinely declare that its aim was nondomination? Ben-Gurion was more sensitive to the problem now than ever before.

Ben-Gurion was in quest of a formula that would do full justice to both Jews and Arabs. In this respect, his point of departure was close to that of Brith Shalom, an association of Jews established in 1925 who believed that Palestine should be made a binational state. This was the same solution Magnes championed. Ben-Gurion attended the inauguration of Brith Shalom in November 1925, an event intended not as a debate between opponents but as an opportunity for "mutual consultation between those who hold like opinions."[16] The inaugural speeches marked the beginning of a dialectical process between Ben-Gurion and Brith Shalom, and the more Ben-Gurion worked to deflate the notions current among its members, the more he was inclined to consider their premises in his own calculations.

Ben-Gurion's objections to Brith Shalom's doctrine were numerous, and he presented them at the inaugural ceremony. His aim was a Jewish majority in Palestine, and that aim should be made as clear as day to the Arabs. Brith Shalom's formula essentially concealed this Jewish aspiration from Arab eyes, "and therefore damages us and does nothing for the Arabs." Whereas Brith Shalom regarded the Arabs of Palestine as an independent national entity, Ben-Gurion still saw them as but one branch of a larger Arab people: "In Palestine there are 700,000 Arabs—and in the neighboring countries, millions more." And at the time—1925—Ben-Gurion still clung to his socialist aloofness, admitting dialogue only with Arab peasants and workers, while Brith Shalom's position was closer to that of Kaplansky and welcomed an exchange with leaders of the Arab national movement.[17]

Ben-Gurion made the same objections after the disturbances, in a discussion with Brith Shalom members in October 1929. The Brith Shalom spokesman on this occasion was Dr. Arthur Ruppin, whose pessimistic point of departure was the impossibility of achieving a Jewish majority in less than thirty years. "The question is this," Ruppin reflected. "Can we reasonably expect to rely for thirty years—a long time in the life of an awakening people—upon British support for us against the Arabs?" He thought not. There was no alternative but to reach an agreement with the Arabs: "We must be two nations with equal rights in Palestine," and he offered the examples of Switzerland and Canada.[18]

In response, Ben-Gurion challenged Ruppin's calculations and insisted that with the right kind of immigration—young persons in their fertile years—Jews could constitute a majority in twelve years. The models of Canada and Switzerland were wholly inappropriate from the Zionist point of view. French Canadians were not seeking to increase their numbers through immigration from France; Swiss Germans were not pressing for immigration from Germany. In Palestine, the crux of the national problem was not the relations between those now present in the country but between the entire Jewish people and the inhabitants of Palestine. "The central issue is the right of the Jewish masses in the Diaspora to immigrate and settle in Palestine." Finally, the Arabs of Palestine were but "one droplet of the Arab people," constituting only seven or eight percent of the great Arab nation. For them, Palestine was merely a "small parcel of a tremendous, giant territory settled by Arabs." And justice had to have its day: "The economic and cultural existence of the Arab nation, its national independence and sovereignty, do not depend upon Palestine." But for the Jews, "only in Palestine can independent life, a national economy, and an autonomous culture be established. Only here can we realize our sovereign independence and freedom." By the plain principles of justice, the Arab right to Palestine was inferior to that of the Jewish people.[19]

Despite his typically categorical rejection of a binational solution, Arab self-determination, and a joint representative parliament, Ben-Gurion continued to grapple with all of these possibilities. The plan for federation that he had presented to counter the Philby scheme had been "the only solution to the labyrinth of contradictions in this country." Yet within two weeks, he had made significant revisions in the plan's provisions for the institutions of the federated state. The mandate would be abolished. Instead of a British high commissioner, there would be appointed to Palestine a British delegate "who would have the authority comparable to that of a Governor General in a British dominion." But his only function would be "the maintenance of the holy places." The federation of Palestine would unite cantons—"autonomous states"—which would enjoy full authority over education, culture, language, and law in their domains. Joining the federation would be a "Council of Federal Union," composed of two houses: a "House of the Nations," with equal numbers of Jewish and Arab delegates; and a freely elected "House of the People." Any amendment to the federal constitution would have to be endorsed by both houses, and the federal government would be elected every three years by an absolute majority in both houses.

At first glance, the plan appeared similar to that proposed

by Kaplansky five years earlier. But the resemblance was deceiving, for Kaplansky had proposed the immediate implementation of his plan, at a time when Jews constituted only thirteen percent of the country's population. Ben-Gurion proposed that the federal institutions be established only after two transitional periods, at the end of which the Jews would comprise half the population. Only then would federal Palestine win independence. It was the first time that Ben-Gurion had set forth so specific a plan for the long term. In 1924, he thought that the period of political gestation would last longer, and argued that "we will be committing a grave historic error if, at this moment, we put forth a political plan which will determine the destiny of the country for generations to come, or even for the next ten years." But his revised plan for federation was drawn out over half a generation.

The first stage would last ten to fifteen years, during which the foundations of municipal and countrywide autonomy would be laid. The mandatory administration would still have the decisive say in the country's affairs, and Ben-Gurion expected that the Arabs would busy themselves at this point in undermining the whole plan. The second stage would continue for as long as it took for the Jews to reach forty or fifty percent of the population. The authority of Jewish and Arab autonomes would be expanded, and the Arabs would gradually recognize the benefits of the Jewish presence in their midst. The last stage would open once "our numbers are not less than those of the non-Jews." At this point, Jews and Arabs would declare themselves allied, the mandate would be dismantled, and the joint parliament with its two houses would assume responsibility for Palestine's governance. This new creation would be a federation of cantons; "each population center of no less than 25,000 persons will be entitled to constitute a separate canton." He did not clarify whether the Jewish cantons together would comprise one state and the Arab cantons another, within the federation.

This revised plan for federation was not entirely original, and something similar had been proposed by Dr. Avigdor Jacobson several years earlier. The interesting twist to Jacobson's plan was that it allowed for the possible admission to the federation of neighboring countries, an idea elaborated on in his 1923 article proposing a "United States of the Middle East."[20] But the first step was to create a federal Palestine, and all of the principal points of Ben-Gurion's plan could be found in Jacobson's various proposals. The key difference was the time scale. Jacobson had drawn up his proposals before the 1929 disturbances, and he allowed thirty years for the Jews to reach numerical parity with the Arabs at a rather leisurely pace. Ben-Gurion drew up his proposal in the wake of the violence, in the full realization of the Arab' national movement's aim to thwart any plan that did not culminate in an Arab Palestine. He also had lost his faith in British staying power, having seen the mandatory administration waver during and after the disturbances. The Jews needed their majority in half the time allotted by Jacobson. "Could we constitute a majority in the not too distant future?" he asked in January 1930, and replied: "Our work over the last few years has shown that it is possible. A Jewish majority within 15–18 years means an annual immigration of 10,000 families."[21] If a majority could be achieved in that span of time, then numerical parity could be reached still sooner. When such a balance was achieved, the third stage of Ben-Gurion's plan, that of independence for the federated Palestine, would commence. The targeted date fell sometime between 1945 and 1948.

The revised federation plan was Ben-Gurion's positive reply to the question that he had posed after the disturbances: "Is the fulfillment of Zionism at all possible?"[22] In examining the question, he did not overlook the possible use of force, the method advocated by Jabotinsky. That doctrine held that if it proved impossible to create a Jewish state under the umbrella of the British army, then the Jews could achieve the final aim with their own army. In relation to reliance on the British army, Ben-Gurion wrote that "it is impossible to last long in a country which we are trying to build, thanks only to bayonets, and especially foreign bayonets."

As to the proposal that the Jews organize an army and seize power, Ben-Gurion offered these objections, which he presented along with his federation plan in November 1929. First, "the world will not permit the Jewish people to seize the state as a spoil, by force." Second, the Jewish people did not have the means to do so. And third and most important, it would be immoral, and the Jews of the world would never be moved by an immoral cause. "We would then be unable to awaken the necessary forces for building the country among thousands of young people. We would not be able to secure the necessary means from the Jewish people, and the moral and political sustenance of the enlightened world."[23] Zionism's moral purpose was not simply a matter of Labor Zionist ideology; Ben-Gurion regarded it as a pragmatic and essential condition for Zionism's fulfillment. Only under the banner of justice and morality could the movement educate Jews to the values of immigration, pioneering, and hard work. An educational process could rest only on moral foundations. "Our conscience must be clean . . . and so we must endorse this premise in relation to the Arabs: The Arabs have full rights as citizens of the country, but they do not have the right of ownership over it."[24]

Ben-Gurion was now a partisan of compromise. He had been driven to this position by fear lest "a parliament be established now against our will," for he had no doubt that it would be an "Arab parliament." From his position that "we reject the transformation of Palestine into a sovereign Arab state," he was led to reconsider Palestine's transformation into a sovereign Jewish state. If both sides were to set aside their demands for sovereignty, this renunciation might serve as the basis for negotiation. Now his task was to convince his fellows of the merits of his plan for federation and to formulate a set of guidelines for negotiations with the Arab national movement.

His plan began to take final form in December 1929. In exchange for Zionist agreement to a Palestinian constitution, a cantonal federation, and a federal parliament and government, the Arabs would allow freedom of immigration and settlement in the Jewish cantons, which would have their own constitution, parliament, and government.[25] But before the plan was put to the Arabs, it had to be put to the Jews.

8
A Plan for Peace

Ben-Gurion's new plan did not take his party colleagues by surprise; they were used to his revolutionary and outlandish proposals. Nor was it surprising that they regarded the plan for a federation of Palestine as a capricious one. In the new scheme, his colleagues could detect three distinct departures from the party line. First, there was the very idea of federation, which had never been brought to discussion in any Zionist forum as a political possibility. There was no doubt that the idea stood in utter contradiction to the founding charter of Ahdut Ha'avodah, which called for the establishment of a Jewish socialist republic in all of Palestine and demanded "the transfer of Palestine's land, water, and natural resources to the people of Israel as their eternal possession." From the outset it was clear that many of the party's members would oppose exchanging this goal for a federation of cantons that forfeited part of the land. Was this not one step short of partition?

Second, Ben-Gurion now proposed to Ahdut Ha'avodah that it negotiate with the effendis and clerics whom it accused of inciting the disturbances. Did this not amount to rewarding those very persons whose punishment the Yishuv and the

Zionist movement had demanded from the British and mandatory governments? Not long ago, Ben-Gurion himself had called for the imposition of collective fines on Arab villages and Bedouin tribes for their involvement in the disturbances. How did he now call for negotiations with the effendis who had instigated them, and for talks with the chief criminals themselves?

Third, a dialogue with the effendis and clerics implied recognition of those whom they led, of the Palestinian Arab national movement, and of the Palestinian Arabs as a national entity. Even if the Arabs rejected the federation plan—and chances were that they would—it would be impossible to withdraw such recognition once it was given. This had far-reaching implications. If a Palestinian Arab national entity did exist, it would be illogical to deny it national self-determination. It would not longer be possible to claim, as Ben-Gurion also did, that the Arabs of Palestine were simply a splinter of one great Arab people with many homelands.

In late November 1929, Ben-Gurion's colleagues in Ahdut Ha'avodah conducted a preliminary clarification concerning his "project," as they termed it.[1] They found it so potentially damaging, that they proceeded with the clarification under total secrecy. At the end, Ben-Gurion found himself alone. Ahdut Ha'avodah was then in the process of uniting with Hapoel Hatzair in a single party known as Mapai, and since Ben-Gurion's plan had such grave implications, it was decided to postpone a final verdict until the parties had completed their amalgamation. Until then, Ahdut Ha'avodah forbade Ben-Gurion from publishing or disseminating his plan in public.[2] His spirit fell, and he considered resignation. He no longer knew whether he should continue his political activity on behalf of a party that failed to back him.[3]

In reacting to the failure of his colleagues to detect the merits of the "project," Ben-Gurion began to speak of "deep Zionism" and to maintain that "there are several stages in the understanding of Zionism."[4] Those who rejected his proposal were novices. Only those with deep Zionism would appreciate his doctrine of gradual implementation of the ideology. The Zionist vision could not be fulfilled in one fell swoop, especially the transformation of Palestine into a Jewish state. The stage-by-stage approach, dictated by less than favorable circumstances, required the formulation of objectives that appeared to be "concessions" to Zionists at the lowest level of comprehension, who still clung to public posturing. As long as they remained novices, the more they were told, the less they understood. At a moment when the Yishuv was yet small and weak, the demographic numbers game was all-important, and immigration necessitated a sense of security throughout the country. Zionism desperately needed ten years of peace to build a Jewish majority, and Ben-Gurion's federation plan, if accepted by all sides, would provide them.

Ben-Gurion prepared to present his plan to the new unified party. Mapai's first conference was convened in January 1930, and Ben-Gurion and Haim Arlosorov sat on the panel of political speakers. Ben-Gurion entitled his lecture "The Political Tasks of the United Party," and he weighed his remarks carefully. The reception accorded to the proposal by Ahdut Ha'avodah had made him wary. All his persuasive skill would be required to win the new party to his ideas, as he had learned during the December 1929 meeting of the Zionist Executive in Jerusalem. Many were now in favor of openly declaring a Jewish state to be the aim of Zionism, foremost among them Menahem Ussishkin. He had even accused the Zionist Executive of twelve years of treason for having failed to raise the slogan of a Jewish state. Ben-Gurion believed that "to this very day" Ussishkin failed to understand that there were "750,000 Arabs" in Palestine and that the country was surrounded by an "Arab sea."

In countering Ussishkin, Ben-Gurion proposed that the Zionist Executive declare the movement's aspiration to be the return of the Hebrew people to Palestine. This was an intermediate position, between the slogans of National Home and Jewish state. But the mood was such that his proposal failed to carry.[5] Now he faced a no less difficult audience. The new party assembled to hear his proposal in closed session, and only accredited delegates were admitted to the lecture hall, to ensure absolute secrecy.

Ben-Gurion took three hours to plow a deep furrow in the minds of his listeners, to whom copies of his plan were distributed. The material was marked secret.[6] He opened his presentation by stressing the new dangers that faced the Yishuv. "After the disturbances, the situation has changed. The idea of elementary, physical destruction of the Yishuv has seized many Arabs—I hesitate to say it, but perhaps even masses of them." The Zionist enterprise now faced a volatile concoction of "political conspiracy, religious motivations, and national aspirations, to which one may add the elementary instincts of the desert tribes." Terrible possibilities loomed in this combination.

Zionism could no longer take the support of world opinion for granted. The impact of the disturbances abroad made it all too clear. It was an error to think that public opinion elsewhere had closed the debate over Zionism with the Balfour Declaration, the Peace Conference, and the agreement among the powers at San Remo to establish the British Mandate. The disturbances had reopened the issue, proving that the idea of the Jewish National Home had yet to take root. In Ben-Gurion's view, Zionism's success required the support of sympathetic world opinion, which the movement could never take for granted because of the world's "eternal hatred" for the Jews.

Completing this pessimistic sketch, Ben-Gurion pointed out the frailty of the Yishuv. "Our historical experience is rich. We will never be forgiven for the sin of weakness, should we even act as angels. We are weak, and woe to the weak! This is the philosophy of history. Bitterness won't help us." Finally, the fears of Jews had been much augmented by the grim news from Palestine. The Yishuv was now isolated within the Jewish people, and future rioters were liable to frighten Jews from coming to Palestine and remaining there.

Ben-Gurion then held out the solution. Within a reasonably short period of time, it would be possible to strengthen the Yishuv in such a way that it could guarantee its own security. This required a Jewish majority. "A Jewish majority is not Zionism's last station, but it is a very important station on the route to Zionism's political triumph. It will give our security and presence a sound foundation, and allow us to concentrate masses of Jews in this country and the region." The last station of Zionism was the gathering of the entire People of Israel in the Land of Israel. But this required a "radical solution" to the present impasse. Two factors could thwart mass immigration: the government and the Arabs. One depended on the other. In order to reach an understanding with Great Britain, one also had to reach an understanding with the Arabs, and vice versa. How was Zionism to break out of this encirclement? "It seems to me that finding a road to a settlement with the Arab people is the decisive political question of Zionism." "The hour has come for us to make a serious effort . . . to arrive at an agreement with the Arabs."

Ben-Gurion agreed in principle with those to oppose all negotiations with Arabs who were responsible for the violence against the Yishuv. But it was a mistake to believe that this response would solve the problem in practice.

> You cannot say that this people is a people made up of rioters, and that we should not hold a dialogue and conduct negotiations. Nowhere in the world is there a people made up solely of men of violence, and whenever throughout history peoples have approached this state, they still were not boycotted.

The difficulty with the Arabs was that they were fighting to preserve the status quo, and so had an obvious interest in promoting every kind of complication, riot, and pogrom. They had to be made a positive offer that would "satisfy their just demands." Those who simply insisted on implementation of the Mandate were essentially relying on British bayonets, and that would never succeed. "Political necessity requires an end to the state of war in Palestine, and that means an agreement with the Arabs."

What were the practical steps that Ben-Gurion proposed to take? Once his federation plan was accepted by the Zionists, discussions would be opened with the British on the questions of immigration, land purchases, and forms of government. Simultaneously, negotiations would be conducted with the Arabs on the basis of the federation plan, with British blessing. Should the Arabs reject the idea, the British would then find it easier to permit more immigration and wider land purchases to a Zionist movement that had demonstrated its desire for peace. As this process accelerated, the Arabs would come to realize that their chance for destroying the Yishuv had passed, and they would have to accept the terms of the federation plan as originally offered.

The delegates were left greatly saddened by Ben-Gurion's address. It reportedly left "bitterness and depression" in its wake.[7] One listener described its effect as that of a "bomb" and believed that it had been "a fatal mistake to allow Ben-Gurion to deliver the political address."[8] The next day, a short discussion was held, in which Tabenkin openly opposed Ben-Gurion, and Arlosorov, while accepting Ben-Gurion's "pessimistic analysis," rejected his "concrete proposal." The atmosphere was solemn. Since opposition to the plan was so obvious and overwhelming, no vote was taken. Perhaps the idea was to allow Ben-Gurion an honorable exit, but Ben-Gurion was not interested. He demanded that the just-elected party central committee meet and decide on his plan.[9]

Three days later, the 26 members of the central committee again heard Ben-Gurion's proposal. This time he did not hesitate to abandon abstract references to negotiations with "the Arabs," and pronounced that "I see no reason not to sit down tomorrow with the Mufti"—with Haj Amin al-Husseini, chief instigator and pogrom inciter. Tabenkin proved the great opponent. He dismissed Ben-Gurion's assessment as based on "temporary" conditions and "panic," and ridiculed the plan's detailed provisions. ("We'll never satisfy the Arabs with three ministerial portfolios.")

Tabenkin drew his arguments from Ahdut Ha'avodah's established doctrine. "Socialists and Communists alike are opposed to sovereignty for feudal countries." The disturbances proved the "immaturity" of Palestine's Arabs. "There is no point in talking about sovereignty with a people that seeks freedom through pogroms." Tabenkin returned to the "class solution" that Ben-Gurion himself once had championed. There were no shortcuts; every effort had to be made to help the Arabs along the road of progress. Social and agrarian reforms were the first steps. Only after the Arabs had become "democratized" was an understanding possible. Ben-Gurion, who had departed from the very interpretation he had popularized, could reflect that he had fallen victim to the past successes of his persuasive powers.[10]

When the vote finally came, only Ben-Gurion raised his hand in support of his proposal. "A tragedy for a great man," confided one observer to his diary.[11] But one of Ben-Gurion's leading critics was impressed by the change that he discerned in Ben-Gurion immediately after the vote. Ben-Gurion was "completely changed . . . as I was very, very happy to see. It was as though the man was transformed. He was completely reconciled to his failure . . . perhaps he has understood for some time now—or maybe instinct told him—that he had deviated from the path . . . perhaps he is glad to have lost."[12] The impression was mistaken. Only outwardly did Ben-Gurion accept the shelving of his plan and the prohibition leveled against its publication.

Ben-Gurion and his colleagues were not the only ones to turn over the events of 1929 in their minds. In March 1930, the Shaw Commission, which had been established to investigate the causes of the disturbances, submitted its report to the government and Parliament in London. The commission exonerated mandatory officials, the Mufti, and the Arab Executive Committee of all direct responsibility for the outbreaks. Instead, the blame was laid on Jewish immigration and agricultural settlement, which threatened to deprive the Arabs of land and livelihood. The Zionist claim that the arrival and settlement of Jews in Palestine brought material blessing on the Arabs was rejected. The Shaw Commission accepted Arab apprehension over dispossession as the principal motive for the disturbances, and recommended limitations on immigration and land purchases.[13]

That same week, Lord Balfour died, and the events melded in Ben-Gurion's mind. The obituaries that appeared in *The Times, The Guardian*, and *The Daily Herald* made no mention of the declaration that went by Balfour's name. Ben-Gurion discovered that on the globe-spanning map of the British Empire, the Balfour Declaration was no more than a speck. "The issue occupies no place in England, while for us it is our very lives."[14]

Ben-Gurion's struggle to alter British perceptions, and to deflate the conclusions of the Shaw Commission, was his first appearance in the political role of Zionist diplomat. In the past, his activity had been confined to the Histadrut and the world of trade unionism; he had made his international contacts as secretary-general of a labor federation. Henceforth, his work for the Histadrut would diminish in importance, and political activity on behalf of the Zionist Executive would command the better part of his talents.

The British tried to put the best face on their retreat, but it was clear that the Colonial Office had gained the upper hand in pushing through a reappraisal of Great Britain's obligations. A harbinger of things to come was the appointment of Sir John Hope-Simpson to investigate the implementation of the Shaw Commission's findings. He had spent thirty-three years as an administrator in British India, and his kind were known for their lack of sympathy for Zionism. Ominously, Jewish immigration was suspended for the duration of his mission. The Colonial Office had turned its back on the Balfour Declaration and was pressing the British government to do the same. Palestine would be handed to the Arabs, and the Zionist dream would dissipate.

Ben-Gurion's response differed completely from that of Arlosorov, who argued that this, too, would pass. The suspension of Jewish immigration did not surprise Ben-Gurion, who believed that "were we only to explain to the British government what they are doing, that this is a stab in the heart, then they would desist. The injustice of the thing cries out to the heavens." He remained convinced that the British sense of justice would prevail. But it needed to be prodded. The Report of the Shaw Commission, in strengthening the hand of the Arabs, delivered "a still greater blow" to the chances of negotiations with them. With that avenue closed, Ben-Gurion argued that "all our efforts must be directed towards war" against the Colonial Office's measures.[15] There was no more room for a Zionist initiative on the Arab question. With his plan for a federal Palestine relegated to the shelf, Ben-Gurion became a champion of the Mandate, and even endorsed Chaim Weizmann's policy, though he did not count himself among its "ardent partisans."[16] Weizmann generally held the Labor government in low regard and did not conceal his contempt; he believed that a Conservative government would never have turned its back on the Balfour Declaration. Ben-Gurion, who now accused the Labor government of "betrayal," found himself in Weizmann's camp; Weizmann, for his part, was out of touch with the Labor government and sought to make use of Ben-Gurion's and the Histadrut's long-standing ties to the Labor Party. The alliance proved convenient.

The need for close cooperation with Weizmann was brought home to Ben-Gurion by a meeting with Hope-Simpson. In early June 1930, Ben-Gurion and four of his colleagues from the Histadrut Executive went up to Government House in Jerusalem, to take Hope-Simpson's measure and to explain the Histadrut's position. The British envoy informed the delegation that his purpose was to determine how many more Jews the country could hold. Hope-Simpson illustrated his approach to this chore with an example. Assume, he said, that the Jewish sector of the economy had 10,000 job openings, at a moment when the unemployed numbered 2000 Jews and 8000 Arabs. Would the Zionists demand permits for the new immigrants in such a situation? Ben-Gurion replied that if full employment for the Arabs was a prior condition for Jewish immigration, then no Jewish worker would ever be admitted. Then the purpose of the Jewish Home is to create work for the Jewish workers? To Hope-Simpson's leading question, Ben-Gurion and his colleagues replied with an emphatic yes. The British envoy, however, refused to accept this division of labor by nationality.[17] For Hope-Simpson, wrote Ben-Gurion, "Palestine is a closed circle, without any view toward the needs of the Jewish people."[18]

But the British government did not seem bent on the total "liquidation" of the Jewish National Home, and there was a chance that a vigorous information campaign might thwart the Colonial Office's efforts to rewrite policy. The aim would be to emphasize the ties of the Jewish people to Palestine, and to convince foreign opinion that the Zionist endeavor brought only benefit to the Arabs. Like Weizmann, Ben-Gurion believed that the creation of a Jewish majority did not mean "the removal of many Arabs from Palestine," but "the introduction of many Jews through development and industry."[19] This was the message Ben-Gurion bore during a four-month swing through Europe, with stops in London, Stockholm, and Berlin.

Throughout the trip, Ben-Gurion relied on the socialist arguments that constituted the party line and certainly made no reference to the existence of an Arab national movement. Before socialist audiences, he reiterated the old claim that the 1929 disturbances were "the fruit of malicious propaganda" and "religious incitement." "But our hand, outstretched in peace, will not be withdrawn even when met by the dagger of murderers."[20] This was the slogan of his campaign. In London, Ben-Gurion found himself, *"much less pessimistic"* than Weizmann. "Despite everything, I have more confidence in this government—and the Labor Party—than in *any other government*. I don't know who is more to be blamed for the situation—Colonial Secretary Lord Passfield or Weizmann."[21] Only in 1938 did Ben-Gurion concede his error, saying "we had an overblown faith in the Zionism of the Labor Party."[22]

But before his enlightenment, he even defended the British Labor government in a conference of workers from throughout the British Empire, where he devoted forty minutes of his remarks on behalf of the Palestine delegation to the affairs of British India. He did not directly challenge the claim of Lord Passfield, that the National Home policy would enrage the millions of Muslims in India and drive them to detest Great Britain. But Ben-Gurion feared that recognition by the Empire Labor Conference of the demand for self-determination in India would bring in its wake similar recognition of the Arab claim in Palestine. He thus found himself speaking in public against home rule for India and pleading that the Labor government be given a chance. The fall of that government would adversely affect not only the English worker, but the world proletariat.[23]

This defense of British rule was to no avail. In July, Ben-Gurion had the unusual privilege of an interview with a sitting Prime Minister, Ramsay MacDonald. Previously he had refused to meet Weizmann, and had turned down an earlier request by Ben-Gurion for an interview, on the grounds that Palestine fell strictly under the jurisdiction of the Colonial Office. Now he hosted Ben-Gurion as a delegate to the Empire Labor Conference, in which MacDonald himself had participated. MacDonald told Ben-Gurion that "you know nothing about our difficulties. The Muslims of Bengal are hinting to us that we must satisfy the Arabs of Palestine. Look here, the Jewish Agency has a rule that forbids the employment of Arab workers. Until now it went unnoticed, but now the business is known throughout India. I even asked to be provided with a copy of a Jewish Agency contract, to see for myself whether a rule enforcing exclusively Jewish labor does exist." Ben-Gurion explained that the Zionists wanted such work to be done "by ourselves." Ben-Gurion was somewhat taken aback, for MacDonald had seen for himself the achievements of Zionist pioneering. Once again and for the umpteenth time, he encountered the inability of non-Jews to appreciate the special character of Labor Zionism when it came to the question of Hebrew labor. On parting, MacDonald told his guests that "you are causing us tremendous problems."[24]

Then came publication of the Hope-Simpson report, dashing what remained of Ben-Gurion's optimism that the severe decree might be averted. The publication of the Passfield White Paper, in October 1930, confirmed the Yishuv's worst fears, for the document drew directly on Hope-Simpson's recommendations. In the matter of agricultural settlement, the documents determined that there was no arable land to spare in Palestine, hence no room for additional Jewish settlers. The Passfield White Paper reinterpreted the Balfour Declaration, by emphasizing the phrase that promised not to prejudice the rights of the country's non-Jewish inhabitants. The view that the commitment to the Jewish National Home took overriding precedence was rejected as erroneous. The development of the country, immigration, and unemployment, were all related problems; by declaring them related, the White Paper rejected the Zionist idea of Palestine's division into two separate economies. The economic absorptive capacity of the entire country would be the sole determinant of the scale of Jewish immigration. And this Palestine, with its one economy, would comprise a single political entity. Self-rule and self-determination would be encouraged by the establishment of a Legislative Council along the lines of the proposal made in the White Paper of 1922.[25]

For Ben-Gurion and company, who had vested such trust in the Labor government, the White Paper was one more bitter pill. Not only did it find a conflict of interests between Jews and Arabs, not only did it take the task of preparing immigration lists away from the Histadrut, but it incorporated a scathing critique of the principle of Hebrew labor and Jewish self-realization. Zionist pioneering, far from bringing progress and benefit to the Arabs, simply aggravated the conflict. The principles of Labor Zionism had been utterly rejected by a Labor government. The Passfield White Paper struck Ben-Gurion like a blow. He was furious with "these cowardly traitors" who were responsible for the new policy.

> England is a great power, the greatest empire. But to shatter even the largest stones on earth, it takes only a small quantity of explosive powder. Such powder packs tremendous force. If the creative force within us is capable of stopping this evil empire, then the explosive force will ignite, and we will topple this blood-stained *imperium*. . . . We will be those who take this war upon ourselves and beware thee, British Empire![26]

Ben-Gurion had no doubt that this Jewish war against Great Britain might finish off the Jewish National Home. Neither

France nor America would take up the mantle of Zionism that Great Britain seemed to have discarded. After the Passfield White Paper, Ben-Gurion began to seek out another partner, in the Arab national movement. His new idea was that Zionism would close ranks with the Arabs, in Palestine and elsewhere, to defeat European imperialism and drive the imperial powers away from the Middle East. Zionism would bear the torch of liberation to the East. Ben-Gurion called on his party colleagues "to prepare for a long and difficult road, if we are left with no alternative, a road of alliance with the Arabs against these despicable powers."[27] While Ben-Gurion issued these tempestuous statements, Arlosorov asked journalists not to publish them,[28] and Ben-Gurion's appeal for war against Great Britain and alliance with the Arabs was never raised in any party forum.

Ben-Gurion developed a "theory," which held that Great Britain would not reverse the new policy enshrined in the Passfield White Paper. But the government of Ramsay MacDonald wavered in the face of the Zionist campaign, and on February 13, 1931, MacDonald sent a letter to Weizmann that marked yet another reversal in British policy. MacDonald reiterated the British commitment to the creation of a Jewish National Home and annulled the principal features of the Passfield White Paper that limited immigration and settlement. The letter renounced any intention to ban the immigration of Jewish workers as a cure for Arab unemployment. Land sales to Jews would be permitted after all. The principle of *Avodah Ivrit*, the exclusive employment of Jewish labor in the Jewish sector, was admitted as legitimate practice. In a word, the MacDonald Letter approved the concept of separation of Jews and Arabs. The Yishuv stood on the brink of a prodigious growth.

Ben-Gurion changed gears once more. He again became a partisan of cooperation with Great Britain and abandoned the notion of a Zionist–Arab alliance to rid the Middle East of imperialism. But Ben-Gurion remained convinced that a dialogue with the Arabs was the need of the hour, in order to set Zionist–British relations on an even keel and make the most of the MacDonald Letter. His first move was the publication of a book of his writings and speeches on the Arab question, based on material that he had assembled even before the publication of the Passfield White Paper. Ben-Gurion turned to Mapai with a request that it publish the work; this would constitute his passport to meetings with Arab leaders. The party's approval would mean that the ban that had been placed on public discussion of his federation plan had been lifted, for it figured in the documents marked for publication. In July 1930, Mapai had not yet given final approval, and Ben-Gurion wrote in his diary that "Berl Katznelson still hesitates." Other party members wondered "whether it is desirable to issue the work under the party's auspices."[29]

These doubts reflected deep divisions of opinion within Mapai about the party's attitude to a legislative council, the most important provision of the Passfield White Paper left intact by the MacDonald Letter. The matter came up for a full discussion in a meeting of the Mapai council in February 1931.[30] The Zionist movement as a whole opposed the idea of a legislative council, but within Mapai there were different views. Arlosorov argued that it ought not to be rejected outright, for he did not want it said that the Zionists opposed a political agreement. Arlosorov preferred to give a qualified yes to the idea, in the expectation that the Arabs would reject it. A considerable amount of time could be bought by such a maneuver.

Ben-Gurion was more doctrinaire and less diplomatic, and he rejected a legislative council outright. The very idea of such a council in a country under foreign rule was "absurd." Instead, Ben-Gurion advocated an earnest and direct dialogue with the Arabs. The events of 1929 had wrought this change in Ben-Gurion alone. Katznelson stuck to Ahdut Ha'avodah's old line of avoiding all mention of the Arab question in party manifestos and policy statements. In Katznelson's draft of the principles on which Mapai was founded, no reference was made to the Arabs; it was Ben-Gurion who added to the document that "the party establishes ties of friendship with the Arab workers, and promotes peace and understanding between the Arab and Hebrew peoples."

Now, in the Mapai forum, Ben-Gurion declared that "we have erred for ten years now . . . the crux is not cooperation with the English, but with the Arabs." By this he meant not merely a relationship of friendship and mutual aid, but political cooperation, which he called the "cornerstone" of "Arab-Jewish-English rule in Palestine." "Let's not deceive ourselves and think that when we approach the Arabs and tell them 'We'll build schools and better your economic conditions,' that we've succeeded. Let's not think that the Arabs by nature are different from us." Labor Zionism, as a movement that aspired for justice, had to recognize its own imperfection on this point and make amends. In the heat of argument, Ben-Gurion turned to one of his critics and asked: "Do you think that, by extending economic favors to the Arabs, you can make them forget their political rights in Palestine?" Did Mapai believe that by aiding the Arabs to secure decent housing and grow bumper crops they could persuade the Arabs to regard themselves "as complete strangers in the land which is theirs"?

"We must find a solution to the political question in Palestine," Ben-Gurion continued.

> We can't find a solution which denies the fundamentals of Zionism. But if there is a solution which does not contradict but complements our cause, then we must use every means to reach an agreement and give maximum satisfaction to the Arabs. Not simply sinecures but genuine satisfaction: participation of the Arab people in the actual government of Palestine.

Only one conclusion could be deduced from Ben-Gurion's remarks, a conclusion feared by Mapai: a Palestinian Arab people existed, and had the right of self-rule. Since another people existed that also had the same right to self-rule, shared rule between the two peoples was essential. This would come about in stages, culminating in the creation of a federal Palestine as soon as Jews equaled Arabs in number.

In his effort to bring Mapai around to his point of view, Ben-Gurion argued that the MacDonald Letter signaled the proper moment for an initiative on the Arab question. His plan for a federated Palestine, in his own opinion, was "the only proposal which the Arabs might possibly accept," and it was important to present it for Arab consideration right away, because the Arabs were smarting from the MacDonald Letter and "might seek revenge." Victory would be turned into defeat. Then, too, the Jews were lording it over the Arabs, congratulating themselves for winning over the British government and world opinion. Just as "for many years we did not see the major political difficulty—the Arabs in Palestine and the neighboring countries—there is a danger that in the future we may forget the problem, until political events in London or Palestine remind us once again." Before the MacDonald Letter, an initiative would have been pointless, for "we then lay on the ground battered and wounded," and the Arabs would not have listened. Now that the situation had completely turned around, "we must now take up the initiative."

Fear of the Yishuv's possible destruction also weighed heavily on Ben-Gurion's political thinking, and he tried to impart some of that apprehension to his listeners. If a political solution were not found, there would be new outbreaks of violence in which Arabs from neighboring territories would participate. On this possible intervention, he had already offered his observations, before and after the 1929 disturbances. Now he expanded on the danger. "I believe in facts," he declared, and these facts were the 600,000 Arabs in Palestine, the 15 million Arabs "in the vicinity of Palestine," and another 300 million Muslims throughout the world. These increased the ever-present danger of physical destruction. Ben-Gurion noted that

> . . . the only thing separating us from the sword of Ibn Saud, this fanatic king who sits a half-day's journey from Tel Aviv . . . is not Ibn Saud's love for us, but British bayonets. If not today then tomorrow, he will arrive here and make short shrift of us. . . . The only thing now standing between us . . . and the sword of the Bedouin in Transjordan and the Arab peasant in Palestine, is English rule.

And for the Yishuv's security, "let us not rely on English friendship . . . let us be careful not to depend solely on the help of England." Lasting security and peace could be had only through self-defense and a political settlement. It was thus necessary to speak with the Arabs. To drive his point home, Ben-Gurion dramatized: "I'll go still further, and say that I am ready to be a submissive slave to Ibn Saud and the Arab effendis if there is no alternative . . . if I knew that there lay the road to Zionist fulfillment."

Finally, Mapai reached a decision, declaring "the necessity of amending the constitutional order, with the agreement of Jews and Arabs, on the basis of equal participation by Jewish and Arab representatives alongside the mandatory administration."[31] Although this parity was meant to apply to a legislative council and not the administrative apparatus of a federated Palestine, Mapai definitely had moved in Ben-Gurion's direction. The major obstacle to publication of Ben-Gurion's book had been lifted, and in June 1931, the Histadrut publishing house issued his collection under the title *We and Our Neighbors*. Within a week, 1000 copies had been sold, and by mid-September 1931, the edition was out of print. This constituted "record distribution."[32]

We and Our Neighbors was the first and last book by a Mapai leader of the highest echelon to deal exclusively with the Arab question. It could have served as an ideological guide to the perplexed, if not for Mapai, then at least for Ben-Gurion himself, one of the party's two or three central figures.

But Ben-Gurion had no such expectations from the book. "This does not purport to be a systematic and exhaustive treatment of the subject," he wrote in the introduction. Ben-Gurion's purpose in publishing was more practical: to convince the Arabs with whom he sought a dialogue, that Labor Zionism had no plan to dominate or dislodge them, but desired understanding, cooperation, and an agreement between the two peoples. Policy, he wrote in the book, had to rest on two things: "on the clear, aware, and courageous perception of the recesses and fathomless depths of reality" and "alert and intuitive harkening for the forces of change and motives of the future which are the heart beats of ever-renewing history."[33] His hand on the pulse, Ben-Gurion was sure that the time for dialogue had come.

9
The Dialogue Delayed

Ben-Gurion's sole preparation for the important task he set for himself—the opening of a Jewish–Arab dialogue—was his limited experience in Histadrut activities among Arab workers. From the outset, he faced the problem of language. In 1909, at Sejera, Ben-Gurion had studied Arabic, but he had dropped the language before mastering its rudiments. Later he invested much more effort in learning Turkish, and achieved remarkable fluency. A thorough knowledge of Turkish also seemed highly practical to Ben-Gurion at the time, since it was the language of government and administration in Palestine. But after the collapse of the Ottoman Empire, he found his Turkish to be of no enduring value. In a May Day speech to railway workers in 1921 in Haifa, Ben-Gurion spoke in Turkish, in the hope that he would be generally understood by the Arabs present. He was in for a disappointment. Only the old-timers could still make any sense of the language, and they translated for the others.[1] Ben-Gurion knew that he left the impression of being old-fashioned by speaking in Turkish, and never again addressed Arabs in the language.

Ben-Gurion had command of two other languages that could serve as media of communication with Arabs. He had an imperfect knowledge of French, which left him far from satisfied. After a discussion with a Lebanese Maronite newspaper editor in 1929, Ben-Gurion wrote in his diary: "I tried to explain Zionism to him, as far as my French permitted me."[2] English, therefore, remained the only direct and unencumbered medium for Ben-Gurion's encounters with Arabs. But, as in the case of French, reliance on English restricted his contacts to the educated intelligentsia, a serious limitation for a labor leader.

Ben-Gurion had an aptitude for languages, and spoke Hebrew, Yiddish, Turkish, English, French, German, and Russian. Later in life he learned ancient Greek and Spanish. But he never learned Arabic and never explained why. When he decided to seek a dialogue with the Arabs after 1929, time was short and one could readily conduct talks with the Arab nationalist leadership in English. Perhaps Arabic no longer seemed essential, once Ben-Gurion decided to pursue his dialogue with Arab notables rather than workers. In any event, Ben-Gurion made no attempt to add Arabic to his repertoire.

Ben-Gurion, then, did not know the Arabs firsthand. What he learned of their culture, needs, problems, and aspirations came to him indirectly. In all his Histadrut dealings with Arabs, Ben-Gurion required a translator, hence his insistence that the Histadrut Executive always employ a secretary fluent in Arabic. This lack of any common language not only prevented Arabs affiliated with the Histadrut from regarding him as their leader, but it impeded all his plans for simply informing them.

His associations with Arabs were hitherto inconsequential and could be counted on one hand. The most important of Ben-Gurion's Arab encounters were his dealings with Philip Hassun, a Christian Arab tailor, who in July 1925 founded a workers' club for Arabs and Jews in Haifa. The club was intended by the Histadrut to be the chief instrument for organizing Arab workers in mixed workplaces and elsewhere.

After a promising start, the club's membership grew rapidly from 60 to 250. For the most part, the members worked as tailors and carpenters; fewer labored in heavier industries. The club's most notable success was a two-week carpenters' strike, which succeeded in reducing the work day from fourteen to nine hours. In reporting this achievement to his diary, Ben-Gurion first recorded Hassun's name.[3] Afterwards, Hassun proceeded to Acre, where he convinced the Arab workers of a factory to join a strike launched by Jewish workers. Hassun spoke in a Histadrut forum of the blessing born by the Histadrut to Arab workers, and announced that "the Arab worker can rely on no one to organize him but the Hebrew worker."[4] Ben-Gurion was impressed, and planned a busy future for Hassun in the Histadrut's service.

But the club failed to live up to Ben-Gurion's expectations. The influx of Arab workers from Damscus did much to undermine the efforts of Hassun, for the Syrian newcomers were willing to work long hours for low wages with scarcely a complaint. In a Histadrut memorandum, this was the reason given for the club's decline.[5] Even before the 1929 disturbances, the club was limping badly, and by January 1929, it had been closed, "for lack of means."[6]

After the disturbances, an attempt was made to revive the club, as a way to breach the wall of Arab animosity thrown up by the violence. Again, Philip Hassun was the chosen instrument. This time, however, the club ran into stiff resistance, from both Arab nationalists and Arab communists, and only a few of its former patrons renewed their membership. At the same time, Hassun clashed with Haifa's labor boss, Abba Khoushy, who thought the Arab club leader indolent and irresponsible in financial affairs. An unpleasant situation developed, with Hassun attempting to play Ben-Zvi and Ben-Gurion against Abba Khoushy, whom Hassun believed was bent on destroying him and his family. In June 1932, the committee within the Histadrut Executive responsible for Arab affairs decided to fire Hassun, bringing to an unsuccessful close the most determined effort of the Histadrut to organize Arabs. The episode probably left Ben-Gurion with a distaste for those whose friendship could be bought, as Hassun's was, and Ben-Gurion became a firm opponent of the technique of overt or subtle bribery of Arabs.

In the meantime, Ben-Gurion established a special committee to research and direct the Arab affairs of the Histadrut. Among its occasional members were Moshe Sharett, Michael Assaf, Eliyahu Sasson, Reuven Shiloah and Eliyahu Eilat. One of the first steps of this committee was to commission a sociological study based on questionnaires, designed to point the committee in the right direction. The ill-fated workers' club also came under the advisory authority of the committee. Although little issued from these early efforts, a group of people with expertise in Arab affairs had been formed, and this fact alone constituted unprecedented recognition of the importance of the Arab question. In 1933, following his election as direcctor of the political department of the Jewish Agency, Ben-Gurion transferred many of these specialists to the department's Arab Bureau, where they exercised considerable influence.

Among the first proposals put to the committee by Ben-Gurion was the possible establishment of an Arabic newspaper. In December 1929, he submitted a request to the government for a publishing license, for a newspaper to be edited by Moshe Sharett and entitled *al-Haqiqa* (The Truth). The paper would explain to Arab workers and fellahs the just aspirations of Labor Zionism and would complement the work of Jewish–Arab clubs. The appointment of Moshe Sharett, in October 1931, as secretary to the Jewish Agency's political department represented a setback to the plan, and Ben-Gurion opposed Sharett's move for precisely this reason.[7]

Ben-Gurion was of the opinion that the Histadrut needed a popular newspaper for workers and fellahs rather than a political organ. The articles would explain the "racial" and linguistic ties that bound Arabs and Jews and refute the "many lies spread by those who hate us." From this newspaper, Arabs would learn how Jews raised their children and crops, treated their women, and helped one another. Ben-Gurion did not anticipate that the newspaper's message would be "heard and understood immediately." He also realized that "the most difficult problem is how to distribute the newspaper, and how to write it so that it will be *clear* to the Arab." Yet he had no doubt that "if we succeed in a number of villages, the newspaper will spread very quickly."[8]

Michael Assaf, whose specialty was Arabic and Arab affairs, tried to burst Ben-Gurion's bubble at the first opportunity. A popular newspaper as envisioned by Ben-Gurion was impossible, because most of the fellahs and workers were illiterate. At best, they would be listeners rather than readers of the paper. But was there any chance that those who read aloud to the villagers would chose, of all things, a Zionist, socialist newspaper? And even if they could be counted on to read the paper aloud, could it be written in a language understood by the listeners? Did the Histadrut have journalists capable of writing in the style of Arabic already current in the Arabic press? Could the Histadrut organize reading circles on its own, to ensure that the newspaper would find an audience? Assaf was pessimistic on all of these points and offered an alternative plan. It would be better, he maintained, to publish a newspaper directed at the intelligentsia, at young intellectuals and activists.[9]

But Ben-Gurion would not be swayed. The newspaper had to be directed to the people, not to a narrow circle of intellectuals. "I assume that there is no Arabic newspaper in the country *for the people* . . . we have a genuine understanding of the needs of the people and the working man." And there were those with views still more pessimistic than Assaf's. According to them, the Histadrut lacked the human and financial resources for publication of such a newspaper, and even if the talent and money could be found, the newspaper would dash itself against "a wall of hatred." The newspaper would immediately be identified as hostile. "The Arabs will say, 'Look, the Jews are trying to divide us.' "[10]

The investigation of the proposal eventually petered out, and only in 1937, after the outbreak of the Arab Revolt, did such a newspaper appear. Its circulation never exceeded 2000 free copies.

However, Ben-Gurion had established himself as an advocate of the direct approach to the Arab question, and he would never change. Arlosorov had no interest in dialogue, and when he suggested that an initiative be taken, it was invariably to stall for time. His aim was not to reach an agreement, but to impress the British with Zionist aspirations for peace; his concessions were proposed in the full expectation that the Arabs would reject them.

Katznelson, on the other hand, was averse to any dealings with the effendis, and he remained convinced that Zionism's task was to erode the Arab feudal order before seeking any understanding. Then there were the Arabists, experts convinced that the shortest way to Arab minds led through their pocketbooks. They favored bribing journalists and anyone else who could be counted on to generate good will for money. Ben-Gurion, in contrast, believed that all men were political animals and that a straightforward agreement on the basis of mutual interests was not beyond grasp. The deal could not be concluded with cheated Arabs, unrepresentative Arabs, or bought Arabs. Real peace, a fundamental aspiration of both peoples, could be negotiated only between genuine nationalists.

At the 1933 Zionist Congress held in Prague, Ben-Gurion was elected to serve alongside Moshe Sharett as codirector of the Jewish Agency's political department. But Ben-Gurion did not resign his Histadrut post and divided his work week evenly between Histadrut headquarters in Tel Aviv, and the Jewish Agency offices in Jerusalem. Although he left the day-to-day management of the political department to Sharett, he nonetheless regarded himself as "responsible for Zionist policy"[11] and devoted the better part of his time to political affairs.

With the rise of Hitler to power in Germany in January 1933, Ben-Gurion cited increased immigration as "the chief task of the Zionist movement."[12] By January 1934, he was moved to this prophecy: "Hitler's rule places the entire Jewish people in danger." World war was on the horizon. "Who knows, perhaps only four or five years (if not less) separate us from that terrible day. In that period, we have to double our numbers."[13] Time, the most precious commodity in this plan for a federated Palestine, was growing short.

Immigration, however, was no longer just a Zionist requirement but an act of salvation. During the next four years, the number of new arrivals increased dramatically. The process, which began in 1932, was the product of the MacDonald Letter and the policy of Sir Arthur Wauchope, high commissioner from November 1931. Wauchope regarded himself as a great reconciler. He apparently had reached the conclusion that a larger Yishuv, constituting thirty-five to forty percent of the population, would have the confidence essential to strike a deal with the Arabs over self-government. The increase in immigration was his concession to the Zionists, but in return, he asked for Zionist assent to the establishment of a legislative council agreeable to the Arabs.

Wauchope was sure of his ability to reconcile the two sides, and bring them to agreement on a formula for self-government. He saw it as his task to win the trust of Jews and Arabs, and just as he cultivated Ben-Gurion, so did he befriend the Mufti, Amin al-Husseini. Ben-Gurion enjoyed a particularly warm relationship with the high commissioner, with whom he passed long hours in conversation. On occasion, Ben-Gurion even spent the weekend as a guest at Wauchope's residence. This personal affinity, as well as the increase in immigration, renewed Ben-Gurion's confidence in British friendship. Between 1931 and 1935, Ben-Gurion saw the Yishuv under Wauchope double in size.

In 1931, Ben-Gurion had told Mapai colleagues that the time had come for a dialogue with Arab leaders, arguing that the moment was propitious because the Zionists, armed with the MacDonald Letter, had the upper hand. Zionist ascendancy found further proof in dramatically increased immigration. Why, then, did another two years pass before he began to meet with Arab figures? It was certainly not for lack of time, for these were years in which he found the opportunity to draw up plans for reorganizing both the World Zionist Organization and the Jewish Agency. And in Ben-Gurion's public pronouncements, the Arab question was accorded the same priority as immigration. The resolution of that question would be "decisive" to the future of Zionism.

Nor did the danger of Arab violence cease to worry him. These were years of sporadic attacks against Jews and Jewish settlements by organized bands, led by Sheikh Izz al-Din al-Qassam. In April 1931, Ben-Gurion confided to his diary what he had heard from various sources: that the atmosphere was one of a prelude to violence on a large scale.[14] In October 1931, mass nationalist demonstrations were held in Jerusalem and Jaffa, and the Jaffa march ended when police opened fire on the crowd, killing twenty-six persons. Police arrested the organizers of the demonstration, including the leaders of the Arab Executive Committee. Work at Jaffa port ground to a halt, and spontaneous demonstrations of solidarity were held in Arab population centers throughout Palestine.

There were two striking features to the October demonstrations. They were directed explicitly against the mandatory administration and not against the Jews; and the Arabs proved their readiness to make sacrifices for their protest. Ben-Gurion concluded that the nationalist movement among Palestine's Arabs had achieved an unprecedented measure of discipline. The Arab Executive Committee could control its constituency, and this left Ben-Gurion surprised and awed. In his opinion, the demonstrations represented a "turning point" important enough to warrant Zionist concern. As he told Mapai comrades:

> . . . they showed new power and remarkable discipline. Many of them were killed . . . this time not murderers and rioters, but political demonstrators. Despite the tremendous unrest, the order not to harm Jews was obeyed. This shows exceptional political discipline. There is no doubt that these events will leave a profound imprint on the Arab movement. This time they really have national heroes, and this educates a movement, especially the youth. This time we have seen a political movement which must evoke respect in the world.[15]

The Arabs "demonstrated their national will with political maturity." And Ben-Gurion offered this prediction: "If the clashes and shooting continue, the fire is liable to spread throughout the country, and perhaps even to neighboring countries."[16]

Ben-Gurion drew three conclusions from these events. First, the intelligence that reached the political department about Arab activities was insufficient and had to be improved. Every awakening need not be a rude one. "The first thing we need is to know the situation thoroughly. We must know what will happen among our neighbors even before it occurs."[17] Second, it was essential to keep up the pressure for immigration. "We will eventually be asked to pay the political price for these disturbances," he predicted. Early in the game, Ben-Gurion came to understand the hidden foundations of Wauchope's immigration policy. To Weizmann he wrote of his fear that the government had set "a specific ceiling on the size of Jewish immigration and our growth." The government had determined a certain percentage of the population that the Jews were not to exceed, regardless of the country's economic absorptive capacity. Now that this capacity was expanding rapidly, thanks to the influx of German Jewish capital and talent, political limits would be set and enforced through a silent understanding among officials.[18]

Third, Ben-Gurion continued to support an initiative toward a Jewish–Arab agreement. After the demonstrations, he again proposed the publication of an Arabic newspaper, as an "instrument of communication and understanding" not only with Palestine's Arabs, but with the press and leadership in neighboring Arab countries. But some of the urgency had gone out of his appeal for dialogue, and for good reason. Ben-Gurion believed that the larger the Yishuv, the stronger the Zionist position would be in any negotiation. And since the Yishuv was growing rapidly, each passing day contributed to the *fait accompli* with which Ben-Gurion would open any talks.

> Because we are becoming a weighty economic and political factor that cannot be ignored or eliminated, the possibilities for mutual understanding have increased . . . far-sighted Arab politicians are beginning to understand that the presence and multiplying of Jews in Palestine is a historical fact from which there is no escape. They are beginning to realize that instead of sterile war liable only to harm both sides, it is better to seek a way toward mutual understanding and aid.[19]

The time had come to clarify the conditions and possibilities of an Arab–Jewish agreement resulting from the growth of the Yishuv. But with immigrants arriving in greater numbers each year, the chances for a settlement only increased with the passage of time. A Yishuv of only 174,000 persons in 1931 was not a convincing *fait accompli*, but the certainty that the Jews would double or triple in number over a few years provided a far better foundation for negotiations. It was logical, therefore, to wait until Jewish immigration gained genuine momentum. Only in 1934 did Ben-Gurion conclude that the scale of immigration created a favorable climate for negotiations.

The delay made still more sense in view of developments in the Arab camp. Between 1931 and 1933, internal rivalries among Palestine's Arabs reached such a pitch that no single Arab leader could enter negotiations claiming to represent an Arab consensus. The discipline shown in the October 1931 demonstration proved transient. The Arab Executive Committee ceased to meet regularly on account of these dissensions, as the rivalry between the Husseinis and their opponents intensified. In December 1934, the Arab Executive Committee, symbol of unified Arab purpose, folded altogether. This absence of an undisputed leadership thwarted Ben-Gurion's practical plans. But he did not fail to clarify his theoretical and public approach to the Arab question. No longer did he leave any room for doubt as to his conviction that the Arab question was a national question, which had to be resolved through negotiations with Arab nationalists.

In the meantime, the Mufti, Haj Amin al-Husseini, gained the upper hand in the contest with his rivals. Even Wauchope began to seek him out. With the reshuffling of Arab leadership, the Mufti's ascendance was ensured. As 1933 drew to a close, and it was clear to all that if anyone could claim to speak on behalf of Palestine's Arabs, he could, Ben-Gurion set his sights on this man.

10
In Pursuit of the Mufti

Ben-Gurion intended personally to "take whatever steps possible to reach an agreement with the Arabs."[1] By 1934, he was convinced that the rapid expansion of Jewish immigration had prepared farsighted Arabs for negotiations. Faithful to his doctrine of a step-by-step approach, he divided the process into two stages. The first would settle the future of Palestine for the transitional period during which Jews would increase in numbers until they formed a majority. During this period, Jews and Arabs would share power equally, on the basis of parity. The second stage, and the final one, would see the creation of a Jewish state as part of an Arab federation.[2]

As his first interlocutor, Ben-Gurion chose Musa Alami, son of a respected and wealthy family, a young man in his late thirties and a graduate of Cambridge in law. Until the end of 1933, Alami had been a personal secretary to Wauchope, and from early 1934, he was assistant attorney general for the mandatory government.

How did Ben-Gurion come to choose an Arab bureaucrat in the mandatory administration as representative of the Palestinian Arab nationalist movement? Ben-Gurion provided an unequivocal answer. He was in search of an "Arab nationalist, who cannot be bought with money or favors, but is not a hater of Israel."[3] Through Moshe Sharett, Ben-Gurion found such an Arab in Alami.

Not long after Ben-Gurion met his partner in dialogue, he sang Alami's praises in a letter to Weizmann. Alami was an "astute man," an "honest fellow whom one can trust."[4] Alami had still other merits. His sister was married to Jamal al-Husseini, cousin and confidant of the Mufti. Alami's wife was the daughter of Ihsan al-Jabri, the exiled Syrian nationalist leader from Aleppo. Together with the venerated doyen of Syrian nationalist activism, Shakib Arslan, Jabri headed the Syro-Palestinian Delegation to the League of Nations in Geneva. The two published an influential pan-Arab and pan-Islamic organ in French, *La Nation arabe*. Both were in league with the Mufti in Jerusalem. Alami's family ties had obvious political portent, and Ben-Gurion went so far as to describe Alami, mistakenly, as "an Arab politician who does not appear as such in public because he holds government office, but who is the man behind Arab policy in Palestine."[5]

As early as 1930, Ben-Gurion declared in closed circles that he saw no reason not to sit down with the Mufti and negotiate, and this remained his goal. Ben-Gurion believed that Jewish "fear of the Arabs, those of Palestine and the neighboring countries," was a major stumbling block to Zionism, and his aim was "to see if that obstacle can be removed . . . by direct negotiation."[6] This purpose could be served only by talking with those very Arabs responsible for the attacks against the Yishuv, foremost among them the Mufti. For just as the Mufti controlled the floodgates of violence, so too could he free the Jews of their forebodings.

This explains why Ben-Gurion preferred Alami to another Arab who only recently had floated a plan similar in its broad lines to Ben-Gurion's. Ahmad Samah al-Khalidi, director of the Government (Arab) College in Jerusalem, had circulated a plan for a Palestine divided into two autonomous cantons—Jewish and Arab—under British superintendence.[7] Because the Khalidi family was also highly respected and continued to play an important political role, the proposal was not without significance. Ben-Gurion thought the plan "interesting," and wrote that "it is important that among Arabs, there are those who seek a solution through agreement and some satisfaction of Jewish aspirations!"[8]

Knowledge of the plan may well have nudged the political department of the Jewish Agency, under Ben-Gurion and Sharett, to support the election campaign of Ahmad Samah's brother, Husayn, for mayor of Jerusalem. But Ben-Gurion did not seek to meet with any of the Khalidis. Despite their importance, the family did not hold the reins of Palestinian Arab nationalism and did not stir fear in the Yishuv. Nor was there the slightest chance that a recognized Arab leader would endorse the plan unless the Mufti did so first. The Khalidi proposal came to nothing.

Ben-Gurion would settle for none other than the Mufti. Late in 1933, still another plan was put out in the names of Alami and the Mufti, which may have encouraged Ben-Gurion to believe that a settlement was possible. The two Arabs proposed that the colonial secretary declare that the Jewish National Home was accomplished and that Great Britain had satisfied all its obligations to the Zionists. The Jews then would have been given an autonomous canton within the Palestinian state, stretching from Tel Aviv to Atlith. An elected legislative council would govern the country, but would be subject to the veto power of a British high commissioner on matters of immigration, land purchases, and security. This plan, presented by Alami to Wauchope in September 1933, clearly presupposed that once the British declared the National Home a reality, immigration would be halted completely.[9] But if Ben-Gurion knew of this plan, it might nonetheless have excited his optimism, and certainly would have convinced him that the road to the Mufti led past Alami.

The talks began on March 20, 1934, when Ben-Gurion met with Alami for the first time; Sharett set up the meeting in his own Jerusalem apartment.[10] Ben-Gurion opened his remarks with the claim that "we bring a blessing to the Arabs of Palestine, and they have no good cause to oppose us." Musa Alami dispatched this standard argument with one quick blow: "I would prefer that the country remain impoverished and barren for another hundred years, until we ourselves are able to develop it on our own."

Alami had struck a sympathetic chord: "I felt that as an Arab patriot, he was entitled to say what he said," wrote Ben-Gurion in his memoirs. From the outset, it was obvious that these would be frank and straightforward talks, conducted by two men who respected one another. Alami struck Ben-Gurion as "honest, frank, and astute." Alami later told Sharett that "it is impossible not to respect Ben-Gurion's forthrightness and honesty."[11] Alami's published memoirs also mention Ben-Gurion favorably, although there is hardly a word of the talks.[12] Ben-Gurion's notes remain the principal and perhaps only account.

For the first time, Ben-Gurion heard the litany of Arab grievances expressed in an articulate way by someone whose integrity he did not question. The Arabs were growing pessimistic. The best lands in the country were passing into Jewish possession. Although a minority benefited from Jewish settlement, the masses had reached a desperate situation. The big concessions, such as the Palestine Electric Company and the Dead Sea Works, were in Jewish hands. The Arabs drew no benefit from the large portion of Palestine's budget spent on defense. The overpaid British mandatory officials were another burden Arab taxpayers bore, yet this bureaucracy was necessitated only by the British commitment to the Jewish

National Home. Arab Palestine was in no need of British administration and security forces. In no other Arab country were the taxes as high as in Palestine. The Jews may have had no choice but to come to Palestine, but this did not alter the fact that the Arabs were bitter. Alami agreed with Ben-Gurion that the condition of the Arab fellah and worker was better in Palestine than in Transjordan and the neighboring Arab countries, but the fact was that the Arabs had lost many of their economic strongholds.

Ben-Gurion did not try to dispel or dismiss Alami's economic fears. He was more interested in discussing the political future, which was the purpose of the talks. Ben-Gurion told Alami explicitly that the principal difficulty lay in the political realm. We want unlimited immigration, he told Alami, and do not intend to remain a minority. "Is there any possibility," Ben-Gurion asked. "of coming to terms over the creation of a Jewish state in Palestine, including Transjordan?" Alami saw no reason that the Arabs should negotiate on this basis. Then Ben-Gurion offered an enticement. What if the Zionists lent their support for an Arab federation of which Palestine would be part? The Arabs of Palestine, even if they were a minority in a Jewish state, would then be linked to the millions of other Arabs in the federation.

After reflecting for a moment, Alami said such a proposal was worth considering. The status of Transjordan in such a federation—whether part of Palestine or a transitional territory between Palestine and Iraq—could also be discussed. In the meantime, Alami did not object to Jewish immigration and settlement east of the Jordan. The idea of an Arab federation could serve as the basis of an agreement, but Alami wished to know what Ben-Gurion proposed to do in the interim, because such a federation could not be realized immediately. Ben-Gurion asked for Alami's opinion on the proposed legislative council and was relieved to learn that Alami thought it a diversionary tactic. The British had no real intention of sharing power, and both Arabs and Jews would be allowed to do no more than deliver speeches to one another. Still, the Arabs intended to agree to the establishment of a legislative council, since there was nothing to be gained by rejecting it. What the Arabs would not accept was the notion of parliamentary parity. Why should an equal number of Jews and Arabs sit on the legislative council, when the Arabs comprised eighty percent of the country's population? Ben-Gurion was reassured, for he already knew that this was an unalterable Arab position.

"I understand your position," Ben-Gurion told Alami, and then he revealed his own plan. "Instead of a legislative council bereft of any real power, perhaps together we can demand a share of the executive authority" in the government. The British, of course, would not wax enthusiastic about this idea, but if the Jews and Arabs were to agree between them, and then present the British with a joint proposal, they could not refuse. Would the Arabs then agree to administrative parity in the sharing of these executive positions? Alami's response gratified Ben-Gurion: such a plan could serve as the basis of discussion. Ben-Gurion would later tell Mapai that "Musa Alami's opinion is that the Arabs will never agree to parity in a legislative council. But he regards the [equal] sharing of [executive] authority as more important and acceptable."[13]

The conversation lasted quite some time, continuing late into the night. Ben-Gurion had every reason to head home satisfied. His two major proposals, for administrative parity in government while the Mandate lasted and a Jewish state as part of an Arab federation, had not been rejected out of hand. The lines of a possible agreement were beginning to emerge.

But Ben-Gurion did not meet with Alami for another five months. Alami became preoccupied with his work, especially with the preparation of the prosecutor's case against the accused murderers of Haim Arlosorov. Afterwards Alami fell ill and was bedridden for a long while. In the meantime, Ben-Gurion met with two other Arabs. On June 15, he met with the Lebanese Muslim leader Riyadh al-Sulh, who was visiting the country. On July 18, he met with the leader of the pan-Arab Istiqlal Party in Palestine, Awni Abd al-Hadi. The meeting with Riyadh al-Sulh was arranged through Sharett; the meeting with Abd al-Hadi was set up by Magnes, after Ben-Gurion asked Magnes to introduce him to a Palestinian leader who was patriotic, truthful, and incorruptible.

To Riyadh al-Sulh, Ben-Gurion presented essentially the same plan that he had proposed to Alami, with an emphasis on Palestine as part of an Arab federation.[14] The Lebanese leader took a great interest in the idea and asked to have its premises in writing. But he also pointed out to Ben-Gurion the principal obstacles to any plan for federation. Which Arab countries were to be joined together? Iraq was under the British thumb, and Syria was still under French mandate. Although the Palestinian Arabs were keen to unite with Syria, Riyadh al-Sulh and the Istiqlal Party frankly saw "no possibility of Syria uniting with the other Arab countries except in the aftermath of another world war."

The idea of a Jewish Palestine as part of an Arab federation was explored still further in the conversation Ben-Gurion had with Awni Abd al-Hadi at Magnes's apartment.[15] At first, the Arab lawyer, a graduate of law faculties in Istanbul and Paris and one of the early Arab nationalists, made a poor impression on Ben-Gurion. Abd al-Hadi had "an evil laugh, and speaks the broken English of a Francophone." It was an impression that suited the stories in the Hebrew and Arabic press about the lawyer's prominent role in land sales to Jews. This "unpleasant first impression" lasted throughout Abd al-Hadi's opening remarks, in which he dwelt at length on the dispossession of Arab fellahs from their lands, as Alami had done before him. This was a claim Ben-Gurion never accepted, though he realized that "the question of land has political value," and he told the Jewish Agency that "we must arrange our purchases in such a way so as not to dispossess the Arabs who are working the land."

Ben-Gurion cut right to the point, a maneuver he could afford thanks to increased Jewish immigration. If you oppose all land sales, he told Abd al-Hadi, then no agreement is possible and there is nothing to discuss. Until now, we have settled here without Arab assent and we will continue to do so in the future if necessary. But we would prefer to have a mutual understanding and agreement. There was no point in negotiating over land until there was an accord on the central issue: Can the ultimate aspirations of the Jewish and Arab peoples be reconciled? "Our final goal is the independence of the Jewish people in Palestine, on both sides of the Jordan River, not as a minority, but as a community numbering millions"—4 million within forty years. The Arab goal, as Ben-Gurion saw it, was the independence and unity of all Arabs everywhere. In exchange for Arab recognition of the Jewish right to settle Palestine, Ben-Gurion promised, in the name of the Jewish people, to recognize "the right of the Arabs to remain on their land, while the Yishuv is allowed to grow through the development of Palestine." The Jews would also use their "political influence, financial means, and moral support, to bring about the independence and unity of the Arab people"—an Arab federation.

According to Ben-Gurion, Awni Bey became enthusiastic on hearing of this proposed exchange. "If by your help we achieve our unity, I'll agree not only to four million, but to five or six million Jews in Palestine. I'll go and shout in the streets, I'll tell everyone I know, in Palestine, Syria and Iraq, that we should give the Jews as many as they want, provided they achieve our unity." After Abd al-Hadi had accepted Ben-Gurion's premise, Ben-Gurion's impressions improved, and "we parted in great friendship." But before parting, Abd al-Hadi asked Ben-Gurion whether this assistance offered by the

Jews included helping the Arabs "to be rid of France and England." For if not, what was to guarantee that after the Jews numbered 4 million, "we won't be left with the English, the French, and your promises"?

Ben-Gurion replied that he "had to speak frankly. We will not fight England. . . . The English helped us, and we want them to help us in the future. We are loyal to our friends." The Arabs, Ben-Gurion advised Abd al-Hadi, were mistaken in seeing Arab nationalism principally as a struggle against Britain. The Arabs should first work to build the economy, raise their cultural level, and educate their people—to give Arab nationalism some "positive content." "All these things are prior conditions to political liberation."

The composition of the proposed Arab federation, with or without Syria, was thus not at all clear. As early as January 1930, Ben-Gurion had set down the principle that "Zionist policy must be in agreement with the British and the Arabs. . . . Without an agreement with the English, there is no point in talking about an agreement with the Arabs, as long as we are not a majority." This principle he reiterated after publication of the MacDonald Letter. The Arab federation, then, would have to arise with British approval, which Ben-Gurion did not yet have. On July 30, he took the first step in that direction by providing Wauchope with a summary of his discussion with Abd al-Hadi. To Ben-Gurion's astonishment, Wauchope expressly asked that he continue the talks.

On August 14, Ben-Gurion again met with Alami, who was now partially recovered from his illness. On this occasion, Alami proposed that Ben-Gurion meet the Mufti, secretly of course. Ben-Gurion replied that his plan first needed the approval of the members of the Jewish Agency's Executive in London. On August 29, Alami telephoned Ben-Gurion in Tel Aviv, to tell him that he had seen the Mufti. On August 31, Ben-Gurion traveled to Alami's village near Jerusalem, to be told that his plan fell on the Mufti "like a bomb." Amin al-

Husseini had no idea, or did not believe, that there were Jews who earnestly sought an understanding with the Arabs. If such an agreement could ensure the religious, economic, and political interests of the Arabs, "he, for his part, did not oppose" the idea. Of course, the Mufti first had to study the plan, which had arisen so suddenly from nowhere. But nothing could be done behind the backs of the masses. Public opinion had to be prepared, and a new climate had to be created. The Zionists had to make a public declaration that would placate Arab public opinion. This was the Mufti's message as relayed by Alami.[16]

Alami and Ben-Gurion then agreed that, on his way to London, Ben-Gurion would stop in Geneva to meet with Shakib Arslan and Ihsan al-Jabri, whose opinions the Mufti held in high regard. Alami would write to them enclosing his recommendation and would inform the Mufti. On his return from London, Ben-Gurion would meet the Mufti himself. Ben-Gurion discussed this plan twice in August with his colleagues in Mapai. There were those who still wished to have nothing to do with the Mufti, but Berl Katznelson strengthened Ben-Gurion's hand.

> When I ask whether it is permissible to sit with the Mufti after the pogrom, in the planning of which there is no doubt about the Mufti's role . . . in order to discuss the prevention of further pogroms, and perhaps even to negotiate, is there anyone who can really say that he would find the meeting itself humiliating?[17]

After receiving Mapai's moral consent for his proposed meeting with the Mufti, Ben-Gurion set out for London.

The road to the Mufti led through Geneva, and Ben-Gurion began his journey with great hopes. With near certainty, he thought that serious negotiations on the basis of his proposals were within grasp. Such was the impression left by his talks with Musa Alami. A few days after their conclusion, Ben-

Gurion wrote to Magnes that "we investigated the fundamental outlines of an Arab–Jewish alliance."[18] Ben-Gurion and Alami were agreed, or close to agreement, on the notion of administrative parity in executive government, and a Jewish state in Palestine incorporated in and linked to an Arab federation.

Alami did have certain reservations. He was concerned about the fate of Muslim holy sites in Jerusalem, and Ben-Gurion was quick to assure him that they would be respected in a Jewish state. Then the whole matter of federation faced the great obstacle of French control over Syria. French opposition could scratch the entire plan. For this reason, it was too early to speak of a general federation, but only of one linking Iraq, Transjordan, and Palestine—all under British rule—into one state.

Ben-Gurion disagreed on this point, because he thought that Palestine and Transjordan should constitute a single state, linked in federation with Iraq. But if the Jews were guaranteed unlimited immigration and settlement in Transjordan, "we will be prepared to discuss a special status, either temporary or permanent, for Transjordan." And because the federation might not come off at all, Alami insisted that only after its creation could the Jews be allowed free immigration. Ben-Gurion, in reply, announced that "we cannnot postpone Jewish immigration to Palestine until the federation is established." Alami would not budge, and he informed Ben-Gurion that without a guarantee that the federation would be established first, "the whole affair will run into difficulties."[19]

Alami had other apprehensions concerning the fate of Palestine's Arabs in a Jewish state. Most of the Arabs were farmers; what would become of them once the country passed to the Jews? They would be dispossessed, "and without land, the Arabs will have nothing to do." The preference given to Jewish labor would then keep the Arabs out of factories, construction, and services.

Ben-Gurion replied that "we do not want to create a situation like that which exists in South Africa, where the whites are the owners and rulers, and the blacks are the workers. If we do not do all kinds of work, easy and hard, skilled and unskilled, if we become merely landlords, then this will not be our homeland." Ben-Gurion's counterargument held that the expansion of the Yishuv would create more than enough opportunities for Arab employment, not only in Palestine but throughout the Arab federation.

When Alami suggested that the Jewish population not be permitted to exceed 1 million during the next ten years—this, at a moment when the Jews of Palestine numbered only 282,000—Ben-Gurion replied in the negative. "Instead of trying to impede our growth, we would do better to draw up a plan to accelerate Arab development." However, Alami doubted whether the Arabs would be able to keep pace with the Jews. There were "no teachers," and in any case the Arabs could not equal the Jews. "Without our help," answered Ben-Gurion,

> you might be right, but if we strike an alliance between us, and invest manpower, organizational talent, science, and money in the development of the Arab economy, the entire economic and cultural situation of the Arabs could be changed. The alliance between us must be built on mutual aid, not mutual obstruction. Our help will be extended to development not only in Palestine and Transjordan, but Iraq, too.[20]

Ben-Gurion warmly welcomed Alami's view that a solution of the Palestine problem could be reached only "in a general Arab framework." Ben-Gurion himself had always maintained that the great Arab people resided in many lands and that Palestine, the homeland of the Jewish people, was populated by only small part of the Arab nation. On this basis, Ben-Gurion had long held that the Jewish right to Palestine was superior to the Arab claim, for the Jews had but one homeland. Ben-Gurion and Alami even went so far as to discuss the possible signatories of such an agreement. Alami suggested that delegates to a general Arab congress from Syria, Palestine, Iraq, Saudi Arabia, and Yemen might elect an executive committee empowered to sign.

These exchanges were brought to the knowledge of the Mufti, whom both Ben-Gurion and Alami agreed held the key to any agreement. In the meantime, the Mufti's only response was to request that Ben-Gurion issue a public declaration, which would satisfy Arab opinion. He also asked that Ben-Gurion take up the matter for further clarification with the Syro-Palestinian Delegation in Geneva and keep all talks an absolute secret. Ben-Gurion agreed. Alami and Ben-Gurion also agreed that the Zionist declaration would specify that the Palestine problem was a general Arab question that concerned the entire Jewish people and that the fulfillment of Zionist aspirations did not stand in contradiction to Arab aspirations. To the contrary, the aims of both peoples were complementary. The precise formula of the declaration would be worked out in Geneva, and only afterwards would the Mufti meet with Ben-Gurion.

Ben-Gurion arrived in Geneva by way of London and Paris and set the place and time of the meeting with a cable and telephone call from Paris. Alami, he was pleased to find out, had kept his word and written to Geneva. Ben-Gurion's arrival, therefore, was expected by Arslan and Jabri, who later wrote that "following the urgent appeals of a number of friends," they agreed to receive the Zionist leader.[21] Did this use of the plural, "friends," indicate that the Mufti had also written to them concerning the matter? In any event, everything was ready for the first historic meeting between the Syro-Palestinian Delegation and the head of the political department of the Jewish Agency. Ben-Gurion was about to bring his reappraisal to realization. He was to meet with two recognized leaders of the Arab national movement, both effendis of the highest order.

On the evening of September 23, 1934, the two sides met in the luxurious apartment of the Amir Shakib Arslan. Jabri received Ben-Gurion warmly as an acquaintance, for they had met briefly at Alami's home on one occasion. Arslan impressed Ben-Gurion as an old and slow-moving lion, still spitting fire when he spoke. After some small talk, they passed to the evening's main event. Ben-Gurion was asked to fill in the details of his talks with Alami, which Arslan and Jabri had learned about in only the briefest fashion in letters from Palestine. For the next three hours, the conversation deepened, without Ben-Gurion sensing that both sides were talking past one another. When they parted, each side understood what it wanted to understand.

There were at least three reasons for this. First, there was the problem of language. The conversation opened in Turkish, but out of consideration for Ben-Gurion's escort, it passed to French. This was Ben-Gurion's first sustained effort to converse in the language, his knowledge of which was far from perfect. Second, Ben-Gurion spoke from the correct assumption that immigration would grow from the 40,000 of 1934 to 60,000 a year. On this premise he assumed that in five years, the Jews in Palestine would number 600,000 souls. No longer would they comprise twenty-one percent of the population, as they did by the end of 1933, but would have reached forty percent or more by 1938. The self-confidence that this conviction gave him was interpreted by his listeners as arrogance. He seemed to them to be whistling before he was out of the woods, and they thought themselves insulted. Finally, both Arslan and Jabri were known to favor the hitching of the Arab wagon to Italy, and Ben-Gurion's appointment of Great Britain to the key role in his plan may well have put them off.

According to Arslan and Jabri, they heard out the arrogant Ben-Gurion, with a growing resentment concealed by grins on their faces.[22] He spoke of the absolute necessity of establishing a "Jewish homeland and Jewish state" in Palestine, which would include Transjordan. This state would absorb 6 to 8 million Jews. Those Arabs who did not want to leave the Jewish state could remain, and their lands would not be taken from them. In exchange for Arab agreement, Ben-Gurion declared that "we are ready to extend political and economic help to the Arabs." The political assistance would include the mobilization of Jews for the cause of Arab Syria. By economic aid, Ben-Gurion meant "investments in Iraq, Saudi Arabia, and Yemen."

Arslan and Jabri made it clear to Ben-Gurion that the Arabs did not need welfare from the Jews yet. Furthermore, to such grandiose, insolent, and far-fetched ideas, Ben-Gurion could not expect the agreement of the Arab opponent. The Jews should go about their business and build their kingdom "on British bayonets" if they could, but they should not hope for an agreement with the Arabs, for whom Palestine was a sacred land. "We told Ben-Gurion that there was no point in continuing this chimeric talk."

Such was the version of the meeting published by Arslan and Jabri in the November issue of their journal *La Nation arabe*. Still earlier, Arslan had described the talk in a letter to an Arab friend. By then he had even forgotten Ben-Gurion's name—so he wrote—and referred to Ben-Gurion simply as "he." "He sat with us for three hours and explained to me and my colleague, without so much as a stutter, that the Jews had to come to Palestine, and that their numbers would soon reach six million," in a process that the Arabs could not prevent. "If this so," asked Arslan and Jabri, "then why do you come to inform us of your irrevocable decision? He said that they [the Zionists] preferred to do the thing without conflict and controversy, and they wanted to emphasize that they did not intend to oppress the Arabs of Palestine or dispossess them of their land." Ben-Gurion's talk of aid for Arab development, Arslan dismissed as "foolish proposals." He ended the letter with this remonstration: "Reflect on the sheer nerve of certain circles, especially among the Arabs of Palestine."[23]

Ben-Gurion, who was not alert to this reaction by his host, actually left the meeting with soaring expectations. It was true that he had heard quite enough to humble anyone's hopes. After he had presented the sum of his talks with Alami, Arslan took a position from which he would not budge: he would not enter any negotiation until the Zionists made an explicit promise that the Arabs in Palestine would remain forever a majority. Arslan also rejected Ben-Gurion's plan for an Arab federation: "This unity is nothing but a dream. It will require another hundred or who knows how many years. And in the meantime, you—the Jews—will become the majority in Palestine and will submerge the Arabs." In any case, even if the unity of Arab peoples were assured, the Arabs were in no need of assistance from the Jews. Arslan advised the Jews to head for "one of the emptier and bigger countries," and build their state there. For any agreement that would transform the Arabs of Palestine, at any time, from majority to minority, was absolutely unthinkable. And if, despite everything, the Jews succeeded in establishing a Jewish Palestine, "the Arabs will never reconcile themselves to this fact."[24]

Then what was the basis for Ben-Gurion's optimism? He felt that Jabri had taken a more moderate stand, a perception that was strengthened when Jabri accompanied him to the train. Jabri assured Ben-Gurion that this had not been the final word, and "the discussion will continue."[25] Ben-Gurion wrote in his diary that "Jabri has a more easygoing and compromising approach . . . he is chiefly interested in the ways we might practically help the Arab movement."[26] In another document, Ben-Gurion recorded this remark by Jabri: "Do not despair, the Amir has not yet understood the importance of the matter."[27] Ben-Gurion noted, however, that Jabri had never contradicted the imposing Arslan during the meeting, and the hints of moderation lay primarily in the kinds of questions Jabri had asked.

Yet so excited was Ben-Gurion at the prospect of a negotiated settlement, he could not retain within him the secret of the talks. On September 24, he proceeded to Warsaw, and in both a public speech and a press conference, he could not help but hint to his listeners about the future federation. When the Jews were a majority in Palestine, he declared, the Arabs would not feel themselves a minority. "It is my duty to point out that there is no historic contradiction between Zionism and the Arabs. *Greater* Zionism will find a common language with the *greater* Arab movement."[28]

In Berlin, his next stop, Ben-Gurion went still further. So convinced was he that an agreement was within reach that he drafted a telegram of congratulations, which the European Council of Hehalutz sent to the Jewish Agency: "We are convinced of the possibility of a far-reaching understanding between Jews and Arabs, and we welcome the initiative of the Jewish Agency to reach an accord between the two peoples."[29]

He returned to London on October 8, and a week later gave a full report of the talks to the Jewish Agency. Along with encouragement, Ben-Gurion also heard a note of pessimism. "Ben-Gurion speaks of an understanding with the Arabs," said one listener. "Everyone agrees. But no one takes the thought seriously. These are merely empty words. If the Agency actually did begin with an Arab policy, everyone would rise in opposition."[30] But Ben-Gurion was undeterred. "We live in the days of the Messiah," he proclaimed.[31] He was sure that the solution to the problem of achieving Zionist fulfillment and reaching an agreement with the Arabs was at hand. If so, his personal achievement, as the one who made the miracle happen, seemed both assured and worthy of publication.

Ben-Gurion inserted the news in an interview he granted to the *Jewish Chronicle*: "During a recent visit to Geneva, he was entrusted with the important mission of continuing discussions to bring about a more amicable relationship between the Jews and Arabs of Palestine. He had a number of talks at the headquarteres of the Arab National Movement in Geneva with the leaders of the Pan-Arab movement." Ben-Gurion described the talks as "very satisfactory and interesting." "The discussions which we had were but in their initial stages, and were intended to establish a common basis for mutual understanding. They are the continuation of the negotiations which have been proceeding in Palestine and which, too, have been taking a satisfactory course." "Permanent and enduring peace will not be brought about in a few days, weeks, or even months—it is a matter, perhaps, of years. There is still a good deal of suspicion and friction so far as the different interests are concerned. But ultimately I hope the efforts for those who are working for Jewish and Arab cooperation will be crowned with success." And the interview was entitled "Toward Arab–Jewish Understanding; Successful Talks Progressing."[32]

Ben-Gurion's vaulting hopes came crashing down on his return to his office in Jerusalem, on November 19. There he found the November issue of *La Nation arabe* on his desk. On its pages, so Ben-Gurion wrote, he was astonished to find an account of his talk with Arslan and Jabri, for they had agreed that the discussion would be "secret." To his further aggravation, the published version was "not without distortions."[33]

He immediately wrote his response, which he thought to send to *La Nation arabe*. In that response, which was never sent, Ben-Gurion protested that the conversation was held on the understanding that it remain secret. The version as pub-

lished in *La Nation arabe* had a number of "intentional distortions," particularly one by which Ben-Gurion was reported to have offered Jewish support for the Syrian nationalists against the French.[34] But it would be pointless to reply, for the real meaning of the article in *La Nation arabe* was that his initiative had failed. Arslan and Jabri's account was the authorized view of Arab nationalism. There was no common language, and no chance to proceed on the basis of Ben-Gurion's proposals.

Ben-Gurion could not but smart from this slap on his face. The nuanced distinction he had drawn between Arslan and Jabri was groundless, and the castles he had built on Jabri's supposed moderation were built of sand. The claim by Arslan and Jabri that they met with Ben-Gurion merely to "know the enemy," that they listened to his proposals with grins, and that Ben-Gurion's presentation was "chimeric talk," added insult to injury.

Instead of turning to Geneva, Ben-Gurion sent the November issue of *La Nation arabe* to Musa Alami. According to Ben-Gurion, Alami answered that he was "embarrassed and ashamed and cannot understand how it happened that they did not keep the matter secret. It is possible that Arslan and Jabri were attacked by some Arab newspapers, for meeting with . . . the Director of the Political Department of the Jewish Agency, and so they decided to publish an account of the talk."[35] But Alami's embarrassment, and Ben-Gurion's sympathy with Alami's words of regret, could not change a thing. Ben-Gurion's Arab policy had not had a shadow of a chance from the outset, and it had even less of a chance now that it had been rejected in public as arrogant and fantastic.

In his despair, Ben-Gurion seized on the publication of the talk in *La Nation arabe* as the cause of the breakdown in negotiations and the end of his Arab policy. In 1936, he would say that his talk with Arslan and Jabri had been undertaken with the Mufti's knowledge, and that "the negotiations were halted after these two gentlemen violated my trust and published our conversation (with distortions) in their French organ."[36] But this explanation could not stand up. In Warsaw, Berlin, and London, Ben-Gurion had made reference to the talk, particularly in his interview with the *Jewish Chronicle*. If the talk was so secret, then why did he mention it himself on these several occasions? Publication was not the reason for the failure.

Ben-Gurion abandoned his efforts to proceed with negotiations above all because of the slap delivered by Arslan and Jabri. Later, when he compiled his book *My Talks with Arab Leaders*, he called the initiative "the experiment that failed,"[37] and so admitted what he had denied in 1934. The whole approach had been wrong. Then, too, Ben-Gurion had conducted the talks with Alami, Arslan, and Jabri in so personal and jealous a fashion, that once Ben-Gurion turned his attention to other matters, no one else could pick up the threads. Sharett, Ben-Gurion's partner in the direction of the political department, was hurt by his exclusion from the negotiation and said so. "I do not agree with your version," he wrote to Ben-Gurion,

> that the negotiations were halted because the two well-known gentlemen betrayed your trust and published a distorted version of the Geneva talk. In my opinion, the negotiation, or at least the contact, was cut off because you then left for America, and had conducted the affair in such a way that in your absence, there could be no sequel.[38]

And so the quickest route to the Mufti proved a dead end.

11

The Stillborn Talks

At the Zionist congress held in Zurich in 1935, Ben-Gurion was elected chairman of the Jewish Agency, and Haim Weizmann was returned to his position as president of the World Zionist Organization and the Jewish Agency. Ben-Gurion would hold this post for the next eleven years, during which he and Weizmann—who were not always of one mind—determined Zionist policy in Palestine and the world.

Since the Geneva talk, Ben-Gurion had had no further meetings with Arabs. As he would later write, "our political situation had changed."[1] He regarded the appearance of a unified Arab delegation at the high commissioner's doorstep, in November 1935, as a turning point. The delegation, it was true, reiterated the old demands for a halt to immigration and land sales and the establishment of a "democratic government" by the majority. The innovation was not in the demands, but in the composition of the delegation, which included representatives of all Palestinian Arab political parties. The Arabs were in a state of coalescence.

This coincided with a change of direction in Wauchope's policy, which Ben-Gurion discerned immediately on its appearance. "There is no doubt that Great Britain today is embarking on a new political course," which boiled down to appeasement of the Arabs, in Palestine and elsewhere.[2] Ben-Gurion traced this policy to the strategic dilemma posed by the Italian conquest of Ethiopia and Wauchope's own notion that the Yishuv had consolidated an adequate base.

In 1935, immigration reached the record figure of 61,854, and land purchases also approached record proportions. The Jews, 355,000 in number, now constituted about thirty percent of the country's population. Wauchope could conclude that the Jewish National Home had been achieved and that the pace of growth should slow, until Jews reached what he regarded as the optimal proportion of forty percent of Palestine's population. They were not far from this goal, and so in 1936, only 29,727 immigrants were admitted on permits, half the figure of the previous year. Already in February 1935, Wauchope began to speak of restriction on land sales by Arabs to Jews.[3] There was no doubt that Wauchope's generous satisfaction of Zionist aspirations, which characterized his first term, would not distinguish his second.

The rapid growth of the Yishuv also produced a turning point in the evolution of the Palestinian Arabs' struggle. Large-scale immigration and land purchases had frightened and embittered the Arabs, who now feared their own transformation from majority to minority. Despite the traditional rivalries between notable families, Arab ranks began to close around these issues, in what the Arabs regarded as an eleventh-hour attempt to reverse the Zionist tide.

The symbol of this struggle emerged in the person of Sheikh Izz al-Din al-Qassam, the rebel, who was finally cornered and killed by British forces in the mountains near Nablus, in November 1935. His heroic death inflamed the political passions of Palestine's Arabs. Ben-Gurion, too, was very impressed with the heroism of Qassam and predicted that his example would have far-reaching effects on the Arab movement. "This is the first time that the Arabs have had a sort of Tel-Hai," he told Mapai, two weeks after the fateful battle.

> This is the event's importance. We could have educated our youth without Tel-Hai, because we have other important values, but the Arab organizers have had less to work with. The Arabs have no respect for any leader. They know that every single one is prepared to sell out the Arab people for his personal gain, and so the Arabs have no self-esteem. Now, for the first time, the Arabs have seen someone offer his life for the cause. This will give the Arabs the moral strength which they lack.

Ben-Gurion described Qassam as "the Arab Trumpledor," and stressed that "this is not Nashashibi and not the Mufti. This is not motivation out of career or greed. In Shaykh Qassam, we have a fanatic figure prepared to sacrifice his life in martyrdom. Now there are not one but dozens, hundreds, if not thousands like him. And the Arab people stand behind them."[4]

At the same time, the Arabs were alert to the crisis of will that afflicted Great Britain in Europe. The events of 1936 and the Rhineland confrontation did much to diminish British power in Arab perceptions. Arab youth movements began to sprout, modeled closely along the Fascist example. Then the fall of Ethiopia and the fear of war prompted an economic recession in Palestine and strengthened Jewish resolve on the matter of Hebrew labor. The economic turmoil, exacerbated by Arab unemployment, helped to charge the atmosphere of rebellion. Franco-Syrian and Anglo-Egyptian treaty negotiations further reminded the Arabs of Palestine how different their fate had been from that of neighboring Arab countries, which were moving inexorably toward self-government. The demonstrations and strikes that accompanied these negotiations left many in Palestine convinced that in the Middle East, as in Europe, violence achieved results. This coincided with Zionist success in killing new plans for a legislative council, leaving Arabs with the sense that British policy could never be altered by legal means, for the Jews had London in their pockets.

In the spring of 1936, instances of violent assault and murder against Jews became more frequent, culminating in a riot by an angry crowd in Jaffa that left nine Jewish passersby dead. From April to October, the Arab political parties directed a general Arab strike, borne aloft by the demand for self-government and an end to immigration and land purchases. The demands were not met, but the entire period was one of continual unrest, during which eighty Jews were murdered and Jewish property, groves, and crops were set aflame.

Did Ben-Gurion and his colleagues in Mapai and the Jewish Agency anticipate the outbreak of the worst violence since 1929? In February 1935, Sharett maintained that the administrators of the Muslim religious endowments, at the behest of the Mufti, had begun a campaign to exploit land disputes, and Sharett knew of efforts "to renew terrorist activities."[5] But Ben-Gurion, though fed with the same information by the Jewish Agency's Arab Bureau, believed that Wauchope would not stand for such violence, and that this resolve would suffice to deter disorders. This view he held until as late as September 1935.[6]

In October, information reached Ben-Gurion about Arab acquisition of arms, a development he found "worrying."[7] But that same month, Sharett told a Mapai committee that "we do not stand on the brink of disturbances and pogroms, at least not in the near future."[8] In December, Ben-Gurion reported to his diary the conclusion of a leading British intelligence source, that the Arabs were too divided and "do not want disturbances. So long as there is no general war in Europe, there is nothing to fear."[9]

The estimate of Haganah commander Eliyahu Golomb did

not differ, and even a few days before the outbreak of violence, he could report that "I cannot say with certainty that the Arabs are planning to cause disturbances."[10] This failure to anticipate events stemmed from the spontaneous nature of the violence and a lack of information on the innermost thoughts and moods of Palestine's Arabs.

Ben-Gurion's response to the outbreaks of April 1936 differed in kind from his reaction to the 1929 tragedy. He did, of course, try to extract some gains for the Yishuv from the events, most notably with the opening of a port in Tel Aviv, meant to circumvent the Arab strike. But this time, Ben-Gurion proposed no opening to the Arabs and undertook no initiative for dialogue. For the objective situation of the Yishuv and world Jewry had changed dramatically. The Yishuv was much stronger, and with the development of the Haganah, it could no longer be regarded as fragile. This new strength of the Yishuv took much of the urgency out of the argument for dialogue.

Nor was there any need to fear that violence in Palestine would scare off potential immigrants, as Ben-Gurion had feared in 1929, for Palestine was now a land of refuge. The degree of insecurity in Palestine as a result of Arab violence was insignificant in comparison with the threat hanging over the Jews of Germany and Poland. These two countries wished to spit out their Jewish populations, and stricter American immigration laws closed the doors of what had been, for many Jewish refugees, the preferred haven. Zionism did not have to attract Jews to Palestine; its task now was to open the country's gates still wider. This reality led to a reappraisal of the Arab question and Ben-Gurion's conclusion that the time had come "to initiate a policy leading to the Jewish state."[11]

For the deepest moral foundation of Zionism was its provisions for Jews in need of a home, and this eclipsed all other moral considerations in importance. Now the distress of the Jewish people tested Zionism as never before.

> If Zionism returns to be what it was ten or fifteen years ago—with Jews entering the country one by one—then the issue of Palestine is liable to be dropped from the Jewish people's agenda. The Jews of Germany must be gotten out of there, and if it's impossible to bring them to Palestine, then they will go somewhere else, and Palestine will become the hobby of enthusiasts.[12]
>
> If Zionism over the coming years does not provide an answer to the calamity which has befallen the Jewish people, then it will disappear from the Jewish stage.[13]

To keep Zionism at the center of that stage, Ben-Gurion demanded greatly increased immigration. To his party, he proposed a plan to press for the entry of 1 million Jews over the next five to ten years, at the rate of 100,000 to 200,000 per annum.[14] For immigration of these dimensions, the Yishuv not only needed British consent, but active British assistance, both political and material. Britain had to agree to a fundamental change in Palestine policy, said Ben-Gurion in March 1936, "a change which soon could turn Palestine into the Jewish state."[15]

It was obvious to Ben-Gurion that the Arabs would turn the world upside-down before agreeing to immigration on this scale. For lack of an alternative, said Ben-Gurion, British help would be necessary to reconcile the Arabs to reality. "The Arab question has only two solutions," he told his party. "One is an agreement between us and the Arabs, and the Arabs don't want one. The other is reliance on England. There is nothing in between."[16] No longer did Ben-Gurion hold that an alliance between the Jewish and Arab peoples could meet the aspirations of both. Plain strength—the growing strength of the Yishuv—was the only thing that could bring the Arabs around to agreement and peace. The support of Britain was important to this image of the indestructible Yishuv.

> Perhaps in another ten years, the Arab factor will be the most important, but for now, the British factor is paramount. . . . The key to the political consolidation of the Yishuv is British policy. Our dependence on British gunboats puts us in a more difficult position, but that is the situation, and we must see to it that those boats protect us and, above all, allow many more Jews to reach Palestine.[17]

This represented a sharp alteration of course. Only seven years earlier, Ben-Gurion had argued that it was impossible to rely for long on British bayonets, and so the Arabs had to be approached in pursuit of an agreement on a federal Palestine. Now, under the shadow of Jewish distress in Poland and Germany, he completely revamped his assessment. In a situation in which "Jews are drowning in a sea of blood, and their only salvation is Palestine," Ben-Gurion found moral justification for reliance on British bayonets and gunboats.[18] But since the British were now bent on "appeasing" the Arabs, Zionism needed to undertake a great political "offensive," directed at the British government and British public opinion. The tragic dilemma of the Jews would serve as the engine of this campaign. Ben-Gurion's belief in the power of British public opinion was profound, and if Jewish distress could be conveyed to the British people, their sympathy would overwhelm concern for Palestine's Arabs and even imperial considerations.

And so on April 16, 1936, Ben-Gurion informed Mapai that he had reached the conclusion that

> . . . there is no chance for an understanding with the Arabs unless we first reach an understanding with the English, by which we will become a preponderant force in Palestine. What can drive the Arabs to a mutual understanding with us? . . . *Facts*. . . . Only after we manage to establish a *great Jewish fact* in this country . . . only then will the precondition for discussion with the Arabs be met.[19]

Ben-Gurion had concluded that there was no chance for an agreement with the Arabs; this was the practical meaning of his statement. The Arabs would come to a settlement with the Jews only after they were convinced that they could not destroy a Jewish state, defended by a powerful army. And that day still lay in the future.

This, of course, did not mean that Ben-Gurion opposed Jewish–Arab cooperation in economic and social fields, but he no longer believed that such contact would yield political benefits. The purpose of this cooperation was simply to lessen tensions. Nor did he reject further efforts to meet with Arabs. But he no longer regarded such talks with the same gravity as he did in 1934; he saw them more as a tactical exercise. By proclaiming a willingness for dialogue, Ben-Gurion could declare before the British that the Zionist movement sought an agreement with the Arabs. Given the political boycott of the Yishuv by the Arabs, there was little chance that Ben-Gurion would ever have to enter such a dialogue. But "the willingness of Jews to meet with Arabs, and the refusal of the Arabs . . . is a weapon in our hands—that is, if the English know that the Jews want to talk with the Arabs, and the Arabs refuse. This is a card in our hand . . . I don't want to forfeit this strategically important position."[20] The willingness for dialogue was simply one more theme in an information campaign now shorn of all expectations.

A few days after his return home in November 1934, Ben-Gurion wrote in his diary that a Jew and friend in the mandatory administration had met with Jamal al-Husseini, "and spoke about a Jewish–Arab agreement (in connection with the federation)."[21] Ben-Gurion seems also to have explored this avenue to the Mufti. Jamal al-Husseini, brother-in-law of Musa Alami, was the Mufti's cousin, and was also one of the more radical supporters of the Mufti's violent tactics. Like the Mufti, he too saw Nazi Germany as a natural ally in the struggle against the Jews and did not conceal his admiration for Hitler. As a pillar of the Husseini camp, Jamal obviously might have interested Ben-Gurion as a possible partner in conversation. Jamal was also a pan-Arabist, and because of the nature of the federation plan, Ben-Gurion preferred to deal with Arabs moved by pan-Arab aspirations.

But Jamal al-Husseini, as one of the driving personalities behind the boycott of the Jews, was no more accessible than the Mufti himself. Jamal, according to Ben-Gurion's contact, had a plan by which

> . . . the majority of Jews in Palestine would be dispersed among the Arab countries. He proposed a meeting of twelve Jews and twenty-four Arabs, to be held in Turkey, to discuss the federation plan . . . [but] Jamal does not want the Jewish delegation to include Weizmann or Ben-Gurion. Moshe Sharett can come (but not as a representative of the Jewish Agency).[22]

Because Jamal knew Magnes, it seems probable that he expected the Jewish group to be composed of those who shared Magnes's views, particularly the opinion that Zionism should concede majority status for peace and limit the Jewish share of the country's population to forty percent. Around Magnes there had formed a group of persons—who became known as "The Five"—who held that peace was a greater necessity than immigration and were prepared to limit immigration as part of an overall settlement.

Ben-Gurion, not surprisingly, rejected Jamal's proposal, but Magnes picked up the initiative. In November 1935, a year after Jamal's plan sank, Magnes invited Ben-Gurion to his home and asked whether Ben-Gurion would agree, in the name of his party and the Jewish Agency, to "40% Jews and 60% Arabs" in Palestine. If so, "the Arabs are ready to allow the Jews to reach 40% immediately." Magnes promised Ben-Gurion that those behind this proposal were "serious and influential people," but he withheld their names.[23]

Eight months later, Ben-Gurion reported to the political

department that the Mufti himself was willing to support this plan, and was even prepared to allow the Jews forty-four percent, provided the Arabs were guaranteed majority status for here and ever after.[24] Magnes, then, did not simply imagine this plan, and he explained the Arab search for compromise as the result of a growing pragmatism. The Arabs had reached the conclusion that the government was a plaything in the hands of the Jews, who could do with it as they pleased. The Jews would eventually submerge the country and take possession of all the land. For that reason, certain Arabs genuinely wanted to arrive at an understanding. Moreover, "if the Jews will agree to the plan, they will be ready to open Transjordan to Jewish settlement, within certain limits."

Ben-Gurion explained to Magnes, for the umpteenth time, that he was ready to meet with Arabs "earnestly seeking an exit," but only on the condition that the guiding principles of such talks address the aspirations of both Jews and Arabs.[25] In short, Ben-Gurion regarded the premise of limited immigration as an unacceptable point of departure for negotiation. This precondition contrasted markedly with his enthusiastic search for Arab partners in 1934. His belief that there was no chance for an agreement now made itself felt.

For Magnes had asked Ben-Gurion to make concessions over immigration, and this was out of the question by 1935. Ben-Gurion explicitly told Magnes this: "The difference between me and you is that you are ready to sacrifice immigration for peace, while I am not, though peace is dear to me. And even if I was prepared to make a concession, the Jews of Poland and Germany would not be, because they have no other option. For them immigration comes before peace."[26] Ben-Gurion left no doubt that he identified, heart and soul, with this ordering of priorities.

Immigration before peace: this unequivocal formulation represented a landmark in Zionist policy. Hitherto, Ben-Gurion had emphasized rights and justice in his Zionist arguments. He had spoken of the just right of the Jewish people to return to their country and restore their sovereignty. The Arabs had the legitimate right to continue to live undisturbed in the land of their forefathers. Because there was no apparent contradiction between these two aims, adherents of Labor Zionism's ideology could maintain that theirs was a movement of absolute justice. This concept led Ben-Gurion to declare in 1928 that "our sense of morality forbids us to deny the right of a single Arab child, even though by such denial we might attain all that we seek."[27] All aspirations could be reconciled. Zionism and Arab rights were complementary.

The 1929 violence started to erode this conviction, beginning a gradual, almost imperceptible process. Once Arab protest and opposition gained momentum after 1929, Ben-Gurion shed his sorely tested belief that no conflict between Arabism and Zionism existed and began to attest to his disillusionment in public. Then the situation of German and Polish Jewry eroded Ben-Gurion's remaining moral foundations. Zionism was no longer a movement of absolute justice; it was, Ben-Gurion now believed, a movement of relative justice. The tragedy of the Jews outweighed the minor dispossession of the Arabs, and to that extent, Zionism remained for Ben-Gurion a moral force. Thus, although Zionism was peace-loving, immigration still came before peace. This was a slogan of struggle, and henceforth, Zionism was to rely much more on the desperate situation of the Jews in Europe as a moral prop. Concern for justice for the Arabs diminished. Rights became functions of tragedies; the greater the tragedy, the greater the rights it conferred on its victims. Few but the Arabs doubted that the Jewish tragedy was the greater.

On April 17, 1936, a year and a half after his last meeting with an Arab leader, Ben-Gurion met with George Antonius, in a session arranged by Magnes. Antonius, then forty-four, was a Lebanese raised in Egypt and educated at King's College, Cambridge. He had left a post in the Egyptian government to serve in the military administration in Palestine, just after the war. First, he worked in the Department of Education, and later he held a position in the office of the chief secretary. Since 1930, he had been the Near Eastern representative of the Institute for Current World Affairs, a New York organization established by the American businessman and philanthropist, Charles Richard Crane.

It is not known how the idea of this meeting was born, or whether or not it was intended to substitute for a meeting with Jamal al-Husseini. Antonius, in any event, was known for his pan-Arab opinions and enjoyed a close relationship with the Mufti. Ben-Gurion even described Antonius as the Mufti's "chief aide."[28] On this account, Antonius earned a spot on the list of those with whom Ben-Gurion wished to talk. As early as 1935, Sharett asked Ben-Gurion to "examine the activities of the Jerusalemite Antonius," and "to get together with him."[29] Ben-Gurion described Antonius as a Christian Arab, "who was well-known as the theoretician of the Arab national movement."[30] He also knew that Antonius was writing a book on the history of the movement, which was finally published in 1938 as *The Arab Awakening*.

Ben-Gurion met with Antonius not once but three times during the turbulent month of April 1936.[31] But the storm then sweeping the country did not influence the course of the talks. These had more the character of an academic seminar running to eleven and a half hours all told—the third conversation lasting seven hours. The words could have been said in another place, at another time. The active participation of Magnes in the discussions enhanced this academic ambiance.

According to Ben-Gurion, he and Antonius were close to an agreement. Ben-Gurion reported that by the end of the third talk, only two outstanding questions remained: the constitution that Palestine would have and the scale of immigration. "This plan," according to Ben-Gurion, spoke of a united

Syria that would include a Jewish "establishment"—a term suggested by Antonius—known as "Eretz Israel," the Land of Israel. Within this territory, there would be free immigration, but the authority of the "establishment" would be limited strictly to the geographic area it controlled by agreement. Whether Transjordan would be included in the "establishment" would be determined in later disucssions, but in principle, Jews would have the right to settle throughout united Syria. The alliance between the Jewish and Arab peoples would rest on the help extended by the Jews "to liberate and develop Syria," and on "Arab aid to Zionism."

Unfortunately, Antonius left no account of the talks and made no mention of them in *The Arab Awakening*, so Ben-Gurion's version of the plan stands uncontested. But even from Ben-Gurion's account, it is clear that Antonius saw no reason to continue the talks. Although Ben-Gurion and Antonius agreed to a fourth meeting, Antonius left for Turkey shortly after the third, without informing either Magnes or Ben-Gurion. "After that, I did not see him again," wrote Ben-Gurion.[32]

Even from Ben-Gurion's account, it is clear that the two men made no real progress toward an agreement. From the outset, Antonius rejected Ben-Gurion's basic premise and held that the aspirations of the two peoples were in conflict. An understanding was possible only through mutual concessions, and the Jewish concession would have to be the setting of demographic and territorial limitations on the Yishuv's growth. The notion of a Jewish "establishment" in a united Syria was ambiguous, and no agreement was reached about the structure or function of this entity. Antonius essentially viewed the establishment as a province without sovereign rights. He opposed unlimited immigration—Ben-Gurion spoke of 4 million new arrivals—and he opposed the inclusion of Transjordan in the territory of the Jewish establishment. Ben-Gurion, on the other hand, wished to include in the establishment all the territory of the biblical Land of Israel, including areas under French mandate. "So," asked Antonius in disbelief, "you propose that what England did not give you, you will get from us?"

It would be precise to describe the exchange with Antonius as academic. It had no clear and immediate political purpose, such as the Geneva talk with Arslan and Jabri. The discussion this time wandered through history and philosophy. Also, the talk of a united Syria could only have been academic, since Syria was under French rule. In the past, Ben-Gurion had limited his plan for federation to territories controlled or influenced by Great Britain, that is, Palestine, Transjordan, and Iraq. Only in the distant future would the federation expand to embrace Syria. But not only did Antonius call first for the federation to include Syria, he excluded Iraq. "There is no connection between Iraq and Syria," Antonius told Ben-Gurion. "The Iraqis were always a people unto themselves . . . and we cannot speak of unifying Iraq and Syria." A surprised Ben-Gurion asked whether Antonius really thought a union of Syria and Palestine was possible without a world war that would drive out Britain or France, or both, from these countries. Antonius maintained that "if the Arabs and Jews are united with the agreement of England, England will be in a position to remove France from Syria altogether." This statement ignored the traditional ties of alliance that linked France and Britain and had been strengthened by the approach of war in Europe.

Indeed, why did Ben-Gurion meet with Antonius, and why did he describe the meetings as a "continuation" of his 1934 efforts to "talk with Arab leaders on the possibility of a Jewish–Arab agreement"? Why did he bother working out a plan for a united Syria when, as Ben-Gurion himself told Antonius, "the Jews will do nothing politically against England or without England's consent"? Was he simply sizing up the Arab leadership? To Magnes, Ben-Gurion explained the difference between Antonius and Musa Alami. "Antonius, it is true, is more educated and cultured, but at heart he is a Levantine, and I don't trust his honesty or frankness."[33] Antonius, too, apparently found Ben-Gurion an unworthy partner because he proved uncompromising. To Ben-Gurion, Antonius had complained about Zionists who "want to bring to Palestine the largest number of Jews possible, without taking the Arabs into consideration at all." "With this type," said Antonius, "it is impossible to come to an understanding. They want a 100% Jewish state, and the Arabs will remain in their shadow."[34] By the end of their talks, Antonius could, with reason, conclude that Ben-Gurion belonged precisely to this category of Zionists.

If Ben-Gurion's aim was simply to learn something of the Arab mood, then the talks, from this point of view, were a success. He came away with a vivid impression of Arab apprehensions. Or perhaps his aim was to send a message to the Mufti about Jewish resolve. Palestine, Ben-Gurion told Antonius, was a "matter of life or death" for the Jews. "Even pogroms will not stop us. If we have to choose between pogroms in Germany or Poland, and in Palestine, we prefer the pogroms here."[35] But if conveying Jewish determination was his aim, then Ben-Gurion had failed. Arab resistance continued to grow.

Perhaps Ben-Gurion had another, more important, purpose in arranging for these talks with Antonius. The appearance of the Jews, under these circumstances of growing turmoil, as patient seekers of understanding and dialogue thwarted by an Arab boycott could only work to Zionist advantage. Readiness for talks was a weapon Ben-Gurion could brandish in his campaign for the support of British public opinion. But from now on, there would be no more pursuit of compromise. The actual talking had come to an end.

12
Immigration Before Peace

Ben-Gurion's talks with Antonius were his last encounter with a leading Arab figure. Later there were lesser talks dealing with specific matters, which Ben-Gurion handed over to Sharett. But Ben-Gurion did not meet again with any Arab representative to discuss the very essentials of the Palestine question.

From Ben-Gurion's point of view, he definitely benefited from the major talks; through them he had learned to empathize with the Arab point of view. They enabled him, so Ben-Gurion thought, to see Zionism "through Arab eyes." He now knew the depth of Arab apprehensions over the growth of the Yishuv, and he understood how this fear led to violence. In a letter to the Jewish Agency, Ben-Gurion explained that Arab fear was rooted in the belief that the Jews dominated the world through unlimited financial resources and irresistible influence over public opinion, newspapers, Parliament, and the British government.

> We have many complaints—most of them just, some of them not—against the British government, and sometimes we think that the government is all for the Arabs. We never consider that in Arab eyes, the image is completely reversed. The Arabs are certain that England is with us . . . for them, the legend of Jewish world domination is a fact. . . . It really is

> difficult for someone who has never talked with the Arabs to imagine the scope of their fear.[1]

In May 1936, he explained to the Jewish Agency that

> . . . there is a fundamental, perpetual factor here: the Arab fear of our power is intensifying. I want you to see things for a moment with Arab eyes. They—the Arabs—see everything differently, exactly the opposite of what we see. It doesn't matter whether or not their view is correct; that is simply how they see things. They see immigration on a giant scale—not just what the government allows, but what we demand. . . . they see the Jews fortifying themselves economically. They see that the Jews have the principal industries in the country: the Electric Company, and the Dead Sea Works. They see the best lands passing into our hands. They see England identify with Zionism.

And they saw the Jews kill the recommendations of every investigative committee sent to study the roots of Arab violence and discontent.[2] To his Mapai colleagues, Ben-Gurion explained that the Arab people were "fighting against dispossession . . . the fear is not of losing land, but of losing the homeland of the Arab people, which others want to turn into a homeland for the Jewish people. The Arab is fighting a war that cannot be ignored. He goes out on strike, he is killed, he makes great sacrifices."[3]

Ben-Gurion no longer maintained that no conflict existed between Arab and Jewish aspirations. He had recognized the existence of a clash of wills very early and had discussed it in his Omaha notes of 1916. But in later years, he denied the reality of conflict for tactical reasons. Certainly collective brooding over the matter could do Zionism no good, and to have proclaimed from the rooftops that Zionist and Arab aspirations conflicted could only have had unwanted effects. The Arabs would have been alarmed; potential Jewish immigrants would have had second thoughts; and for some, world opinion would have judged Zionism to be based on injustice and dispossession.

But by May 1936, after his talks with Antonius, Ben-Gurion was willing to concede the existence of a conflict for the first time in public. "There is a conflict, a great conflict," not in the economic but in the political realm. "There is a fundamental conflict. We and they want the same thing: We both want Palestine. And that is the fundamental conflict."[4] Over no issue was that conflict so severe as the question of immigration.

> Arab leaders see no value in the economic dimension of the country's development, and while they will concede that our immigration has brought material blessing to Palestine, they nonetheless contend—and from the Arab point of view, they are right—that they want neither the honey nor the bee sting.[5]

Ben-Gurion went still further, and suggested that "we ourselves, by our very presence and progress here, have nurtured the Arab nationalist movement." Such a movement would have arisen anyway—the whole world was seething with "nationalist turmoil"—but Zionism had a stimulating effect.[6] There was a dialectical process at work here. Ben-Gurion now realized that, for the Arabs, Zionism cut both ways. It was a blessing and a curse; it sought brotherhood and cooperation but in its wake brought war, destruction, and loss of life.

Ben-Gurion also took a different view of the violence that erupted in 1936. He did, of course, try to draw every possible benefit from its effects, as he had done on earlier occasions. "The first and principal lesson of these disturbances, if we haven't learned it already, is that we must free ourselves from all economic dependence on the Arabs. . . . Not a few victims fell in Jaffa because of this unnecessary and unjustifiable dependence."[7] "Economic freedom means a Jewish port," Ben-Gurion concluded. "If we want Hebrew redemption, 100%, then we must have a 100% Hebrew settlement, a 100% Hebrew farm, and a 100% Hebrew port."[8]

And so in May 1936, the port of Tel Aviv opened, an important step toward Jewish economic independence. But no longer did Ben-Gurion regard Arab violence as a threat to the very existence of the Yishuv, as he believed it had been in 1929. "Since 1929, the Yishuv has grown and dug in. It is no easy or sure thing to do battle with it, hand-to-hand. . . . This quantitative and qualitative expansion has made any repetition of the pogroms of 1929 almost impossible."[9] By 1936, Ben-Gurion no longer feared for the Yishuv's survival, and that confidence later played a decisive role in his decision to proclaim the State of Israel in 1948.

In another significant reappraisal, Ben-Gurion did not hold the mandatory administration responsible for the outbreak or spread of the Arab Revolt. In 1920, 1921, 1922, and 1929, Ben-Gurion apportioned this or that measure of blame to those British authorities responsible for preserving order. But now he argued that "no government in the world can prevent individual terror . . . when a people is fighting for its land, it is not easy to prevent such acts."[10] Nor did he criticize British displays of leniency: "I see why the government feels the need to show leniency towards the Arabs . . . it is not easy to suppress a popular movement strictly by the use of force."[11] This attitude stemmed from his appraisal of the violence as a nationalist rebellion; these were not simply Arab "riots," or the work of hooligans. "Do they not seek to alter the regime by force? In Hebrew we call this revolt and rebellion." An appreciation of the effects of Jewish immigration thus led Ben-Gurion to regard the Arab Revolt as a nationalist uprising. "Were I an Arab," Ben-Gurion wrote to Sharett in 1937,

> . . . an Arab with nationalist political consciousness . . . I would rise up against an immigration liable sometime in the

> future to hand the country and all of its Arab inhabitants over to Jewish rule. What Arab cannot do his math and understand that immigration at the rate of 60,000 a year means a Jewish state in all of Palestine?[12]

If this was the case—if the Arabs would not agree to a Jewish majority and the Jewish immigration that would create it—then there was no chance for peace between the Arabs and the Zionists. Ben-Gurion reached this conclusion even before the outbreak of the Arab Revolt. The conviction grew deeper over the next two years and inspired his declaration that "immigration comes before peace." Ben-Gurion rejected all of the many proposals floated during the Arab Revolt by Jew and Arab alike, for an agreement based on a limitation of immigration. He even opposed negotiations conditional on a temporary suspension of the influx. On this question, he clashed with Weizmann, who believed, like many others, that Zionism would recoup any losses incurred by restrictions on immigration, once the general strike and violence were ended. To sustain his point of view, Ben-Gurion assumed British support for the Yishuv's continued growth in security. "Securing the help of England at this moment, is more important than negotiation with the Arabs."[13]

> We do not seek an agreement with the Arabs in order to secure the peace. Of course we regard peace as an essential thing. It is impossible to build up the country in a state of permanent warfare. But peace for us is a means and not an end. The end is the fulfillment of Zionism, complete and total fulfillment of Zionism in its maximum scope. Only for this reason do we need peace, and do we need an agreement.[14]

In all of his assessments, Ben-Gurion found himself at odds with his party colleagues, just as he had been when he first proposed a federated Palestine.[15] Berl Katznelson did not appreciate Arab apprehensions, did not accept the Arab national movement as a popular expression, did not see Arab violence as nationalist war or rebellion, and did not regard reliance on Great Britain as the pillar of zionist policy. Katznelson's views were shared by the party's other leading lights, Itzhak Tabenkin and Moshe Beilinson. They all adhered to the doctrine of Ahdut Ha'avodah, which had gained currency in the 1920s and which Ben-Gurion himself had helped to formulate. Katznelson still regarded Arab violence as the work of agitators and a perfidious British administration. If the government had only taken a tough stand from the outset, the situation would not have deteriorated into a general strike, and there would have been no bloody assaults, for there was no Arab national movement. "Can this be described as nationalism? Let's not believe it for a moment!" By his standards, the Arabs had nothing like a movement for national liberation: "Where is the *social and progressive content* which we saw in the liberation movements of Poland and of the Czechs, in the protracted struggle against European rule in India and among all those who seek to liberate their culture? Not a trace." Needless to say, Katznelson rejected Ben-Gurion's view of Sheikh Izz al-Din al-Qassam as an "Arab Trumpeldor." "In all these terroristic manifestations, one might find evidence of personal dedication to religious fanaticism and xenophobia, but we cannot discern anything else."[16] Katznelson, thus, judged the Arab movement according to its content and not its political ability to mobilize the masses.

To Ben-Gurion, this was plain blindness.

> There are comrades among us who only see one enemy: the government. In their opinion, there is no uprising or revolt by the Arabs. . . . I have a hard time understanding the astonishing blindness of people like Beilinson, Tabenkin, Kaplan and others. . . . I cannot understand the strange satisfaction which they derive from hanging the blame solely around the neck of the [British] government.

Among the others, Ben-Gurion certainly included Katznelson, who went unnamed only out of courtesy. Now Ben-Gurion went to lengths to distance himself from the old interpretations that he himself had made popular more than a decade earlier. In June 1936, he told Mapai: "At the Ahdut Ha'avodah convention in Ein Harod, I said that we must have nothing to do with the Arab effendis. I would not say that today."[17] Before the Histadrut, he went still further, in February 1937: "I want to point out a mistake which I made . . . thirteen years ago . . . in Ein Harod. . . . Today I would not say that the only way to an understanding is through the Arab worker. We must find a way to the whole Arab people . . . by contact and negotiations with its representatives, whoever they may be."[18] It was one of the only times in his political career that Ben-Gurion confessed to an error. But he made no apologies, for the "mistake" had been intentional, a tactical move to avoid conceding the existence of national conflict between Arab and Jew.

Ben-Gurion had come far in his understanding of the Arabs. In February 1937, he was on the brink of an even more far-reaching conclusion: that the Arabs of Palestine were a separate people, distinct from other Arabs and deserving of self-determination. "The right which the Arabs in Palestine have is one due to the inhabitants of any country . . . because they live here, and not because they are Arabs. . . . The Arab inhabitants of Palestine should enjoy all the rights of citizens and all political rights, not only as individuals, but as a national community, just like the Jews."[19] This was very close to recognition of the Arabs of Palestine as a nation unto themselves. Only one consideration restrained Ben-Gurion from abandoning his earlier view that Palestine's Arabs were but a fragment of the great Arab people. The desperate plight of European Jewry stayed his pen and tongue. He could not surrender his claim that Palestine was dearer to the Jews than to the Arabs as their only homeland at a moment when so many Jews were in need of refuge. Katznelson, of course, opposed any view of the country's Arabs as a distinct nation, and when he spoke of Arabs, it was difficult to tell whether he meant those of Palestine, Syria, or Iraq, or all of them at once. Yet perhaps he, too, sensed in his own pragmatic way that to admit the existence of a Palestinian Arab people was to plunge the Zionist movement and Mapai into ideological chaos.

In Ben-Gurion's discussion of his "mistake" at Ein Harod, something seemed amiss nonetheless. If he had indeed arrived at the conclusion that an agreement between Jews and Arabs did not have a chance, then why did he still declare that "we must find a way to the whole Arab people . . . by contact and negotiations with its representatives, whoever they may be"? Ben-Gurion sought to resolve this contradiction, which he himself recognized. In May 1936, he had decided that peace was impossible: "We and they want the same thing: We both want Palestine." "I now say something which contradicts the theory which I once had on this question. At one time, I thought an agreement was possible."[20] Ben-Gurion attached some reservations to this statement. A settlement might be possible between both peoples in the widest sense, between the entire Jewish people and the entire Arab people. But such an agreement could be achieved only "once they despair of preventing a Jewish Palestine."[21] Peace was not absolutely impossible, but it would come only after a lengthy process of Arab disillusionment with attempts to destroy the Yishuv.

The only terms that Ben-Gurion was prepared to consider were for a five-year limit on immigration at the level of 60,000 newcomers a year. "Below this minimum we cannot go, and if there is no agreement over this minimum, then there is no agreement at all."[22] Yet Ben-Gurion must have known that the Arabs would never consent to this proposal, for he himself had asked "what Arab cannot do his math and understand that immigration at the rate of 60,000 a year means a Jewish state in all of Palestine?"[23] His conclusion was that agreement was impossible. For party political purposes, however, he sometimes had to make other noises, as when addressing Hashomer Hatzair, a partner in the Labor Movement, on his belief in the possibilities for a peaceful settlement.[24] He also had to declare peace possible in his confrontation with the Revisionists, who publicly declared that the Arabs would never relent in their war against Zionism. But Ben-Gurion himself had no illusions, and though he declared openly that peace was a possibility, to intimate company he explained it was a distant one.

He thought he knew the reasons that his own talks had failed:

> First, there is our weakness. We are not strong enough in the perception of the other side to constitute worthwhile allies. . . . Second . . . the weakness of the Arab national movement. The fact that there still is no unified movement, but rival gangs belonging to families . . . spoils every attempt at Jewish–Arab agreement . . . Third is the ambiguous stand of the decisive factor: the British factor. One can hardly say that the government of Palestine has shown much determination to reconcile Jews and Arabs.[25]

The only way to overcome that Jewish weakness, and to make the Yishuv a desirable ally, was to strengthen the Yishuv with British support. That would take some time. "A few more years will pass until our own strength will suffice us to withstand the Arab world which surrounds Palestine on all sides. Until then, we require assistance and a prop from the outside. But who will stand by the Jewish people?"[26] Only Great Britain. British support at this stage was "more important than our negotiating with the Arabs . . . and this will continue to be our principal concern in the future."[27]

His policy toward the Arab question was hereafter dominated by his determination to find favor and support in Great Britain. The talk of reaching out to the Arabs at a moment when Ben-Gurion knew that such a dialogue must be sterile was intended to convince British public opinion and British officials that Zionists actively sought peace. For the same reason, Ben-Gurion again began to emphasize the theme of nondomination. And above all, he developed the policy of self-restraint (*havlaga*) in the face of Arab attacks.

From the very first day of violence, Ben-Gurion understood that the Arab techniques of waging this war could be turned to the advantage of Zionists in winning British public support. In his diary, he recorded that the passage of the Arab banner to the mob represented "a great political disaster for Arab policy," for this "besmirches the Arabs in the eyes of British and world public opinion."[28] The basic principle of *havlaga* was avoidance of any Jewish reprisal for Arab attacks. The Jews would limit themselves to measures of self-defense. Ben-Gurion had valued self-restraint of this sort from his Sejera days, when revenge would have brought senseless escalation: "We learned not to spill blood under the greatest of provocations . . . because otherwise, the chain is endless. They kill one; we kill two; then they return and kill another four."[29] In 1929, Ben-Gurion declared that "self-defense is our right and obligation . . . but any abuse of this right is a violation of the holy of holies . . . our strength is in the purity of our aspirations and the justice of our deeds . . . and we must fight with all our moral and public force against nationalist incitement and displays of hostility from our side."[30] Had the Revisionists only shown self-restraint over the matter of the Western Wall, "the entire history of 1929 might have been different."[31]

From the very outset, Ben-Gurion's reaction to the 1936 violence emphasized the principle of self-restraint.

> I fear that those who today murdered our people in an ambush not only plotted to murder some Jews, but intended

> to provoke us, to push us into acting as they have, and turning the country red with blood. The Arabs stand to gain from such a development. They want the country to be in a state of perpetual pogrom.[32]
>
> Any further bloodshed [caused by Jews] will only bring political advantage to the Arabs and will harm us.[33]

For Ben-Gurion recognized that a double standard was at play here:

> We are not Arabs, and others measure us by a different standard, which doesn't allow so much as a hairsbreadth of deviation . . . our instruments of war are different from those of the Arabs, and only our own instruments can guarantee our victory. Our strength is in defense . . . and this strength will give us a political victory if England and the world know that we are defending ourselves rather than attacking.[34]

Three years later, once peace had returned to the country for a time, Ben-Gurion reflected that it had been this self-restraint that allowed the British in good conscience to arm the Yishuv.[35]

There were, of course, those who criticized the policy of *havlaga*. The Arabs, some claimed, interpreted Jewish self-restraint as weakness. The British, said others, would give in to the most aggressive side. Even Ben-Gurion himself described *havlaga* as a "stupid name" and instead proposed *haganah atzmit*—self-defense. "We only defend ourselves, and do not take revenge."[36] What he said in the argument over *havlaga* indicate a man at odds with himself. Arab terror, which did not discriminate between the armed and the defenseless, among them old men, women, and children, cried out for revenge. In July 1936, after he sailed from Jaffa to London, he wrote in his diary:

> I have never felt hatred for Arabs, and their pranks have never stirred the desire for revenge in me. But I would wel-

> come the destruction of Jaffa, port and city. Let it come; it would be for the better. This city, which grew fat from Jewish immigration and settlement, deserves to be destroyed for having waved an axe at those who built her and made her prosper. If Jaffa went to hell, I would not count myself among the mourners.[37]

But this was no more than a shot fired in anger. It was not a policy. His view of the Arab "above all as a man" remained his guiding principle in appealing for self-restraint and limiting the Yishuv to self-defense.

The techniques of the Arabs could not serve the aims of the Jews. Ben-Gurion spelled out this conclusion in detail.[38] First, the Arabs wanted to be rid of the Mandate, the National Home, and the Yishuv. The Zionists, in contrast, desired a continuation of the Mandate, "and we have no desire to be rid of the Arabs." Second, the Arabs, who were already found in large numbers in Palestine and the neighboring countries, did not demand Arab immigration and did not need the help of Britain or any sort of foreign rule. But most Jews were still abroad. So the Jews were interested in changing the status quo and transforming political and economic conditions in such a way as to make mass Jewish immigration possible. To do so, "we need foreign, external rule, to defend us and promote our immigration." Third, the Arabs could achieve their goals "only through revolt and rebellion," while for the Jews, the opposite was the case. Revolt and terror would not encourage Britain to transform Palestine into a Jewish country. Jewish counterterror would only feed the flames that would likely consume the entire Zionist enterprise in a terrible conflagration. Ben-Gurion concluded that the different aims of Arab and Jews necessitated utterly different means. "What we wish to achieve requires the help of the British; what the Arabs wish to achieve requires war against Great Britain."[39]

The achievements of the *havlaga* policy in winning the

support of British public opinion were impressive. They certainly made it possible for the British to expand the Jewish security forces under their supervision and to arm Jewish settlements from government armories. The Yishuv emerged from the Arab Revolt strengthened militarily. In 1938, Ben-Gurion could tell Mapai that "in the national war which the Arabs declared against us . . . we followed a certain line, one of self-defense, and this line stood us well. We could not prevent casualties . . . but we prevented a political disaster."[40]

13
Peace Through Strength

In October 1936, the Arab Higher Committee called off the general strike, in response to an appeal by the kings of Saudi Arabia and Iraq, the Amir of Transjordan, and the Imam of Yemen. The first stage of the Arab Revolt thus came to a close. The strike had been on its last legs anyway, because the Arabs themselves had begun to hurt from the economic effects of closed ports, businesses, and industries. The appeal by the Arab rulers allowed the Palestinian Arab leadership a respectable exit from the impasse. This face-saving gesture was the handiwork of George Rendel, head of the Eastern Department at the Foreign Office. Ben-Gurion was certain that the timely intervention had bailed out the Arab Higher Committee, because the strike stood on the brink of total failure when the appeal was published.

One might have thought that Ben-Gurion would have welcomed the intervention of the Arab rulers. After all, Ben-Gurion had long claimed that the Arabs of Palestine were but a small part of the greater Arab people and that a solution to the problem of Palestine could be found only "in the general Arab framework." His federation plan had been predicated on the solidarity of Palestine's Arabs with other Arabs, whose independence they would regard as the fulfillment of their own political aspirations. For the same reason, Ben-Gurion declared his preference for dialogue with "pan-Arab patriots," for "only with them is there a chance for understanding and agreement." Why, then, did Ben-Gurion attack Rendel's diplomacy and label Rendel himself an "outright anti-Semite" and "our greatest hater in the Foreign Office"?[1]

Ben-Gurion now realized that pan-Arabism could cut both ways and that the Arabs were in fact more likely to unite in order to oppose Jewish aspirations than to embrace them. Thus, from the outset Ben-Gurion opposed the intervention, in which he saw a twofold danger. First, the simple recognition of other Arab countries as a party with the right to intervene in the affairs of Palestine undermined the foundations of the Balfour Declaration and the Mandate. Second, the ending of the strike and accompanying violence with the help of the Arab kings left the British indebted to them, morally if not politically, and that debt was bound to be paid in the coin of Jewish immigration.[2]

Zionism, therefore, faced "not only a Palestinian Arab front, but a pan-Arab front . . . which is active, and to some measure is recognized by those who rule Palestine." Ben-Gurion thought this the most serious danger faced by Zionism in eighteen years of struggle against the Arabs and hostile British officialdom. The neighboring Arab countries were now in a "position to intervene . . . and to set the course in Palestine's affairs." Together with Britain, the Arab kings would form an "Anglo–Arab condominium" over Palestine.[3] In short, Britain was again seeking an exit from the Mandate, a quest begun with the Passfield White Paper and postponed but temporarily by the MacDonald Letter.

Needless to say, Ben-Gurion expected nothing but the worst from the Royal Commission slated to visit Palestine. Nothing good had ever issued from an investigative commission sent to the country in the wake of Arab violence, and the extensive authority vested in this new commission, under Lord William Robert Peel, filled Ben-Gurion with dread. He was certain that the Peel Commission would recommend a trimming of Jewish rights in Palestine, with an eye toward preventing the emergence of a Jewish majority.[4] The ceremonious dispatch and deliberations of the commissioners were simply to prepare public opinion to accept a policy already decided on elsewhere.[5] Particularly ominous was a sudden reduction in the number of immigration certificates issued in appeasement of or reward to the Arabs for having stopped their strike. A double surprise thus awaited Ben-Gurion in the recommendations of the Peel Commission. Not only did several of the commissioners show a genuine sympathy for Zionism, but the commission considered a proposal to divide Palestine into a Jewish state, an Arab state, and an area to remain under British mandate. In the final report, published in July 1937, the Peel Commission unanimously recommended the solution of partition to the question of Palestine.

When Weizmann learned that the Royal Commission was moving toward partition, half a year before publication of the commission's report, he told his private secretary that "the long toil of his life was at last crowned with success." After a meeting with one of the commissioners, Professor Reginald Coupland, Weizmann proclaimed that "today we laid the basis for the Jewish state."[6] But at this point in his life, Weizmann had not toiled at all for partition.

Ben-Gurion, on the other hand, could well have claimed the success. The idea of partition was inherent in his very conception of Zionism, and it found myriad expressions over the years. The concept of *Avodah Ivrit*, and the sorting out of Arabs and Jews into two separate national frameworks in agriculture and industry, represented a kind of partition. His autonomy plan of the 1920s, with its emphasis on Jewish settlement in contiguous blocs, amounted to geographic partition. When he proposed his federation plan in 1929, he nearly gave the proposal the name of partition. In short, Ben-Gurion's thoughts and actions laid the foundations for a Jewish state to be established in part of Palestine. So similar were Ben-Gurion's plans and the recommendations of the Peel Commission that they almost seemed like the work of one hand.

And so it was not surprising that Ben-Gurion showed immediate enthusiasm for the partition plan on first hearing of it from Weizmann. He had hardly heard the words before he was urging that "we must win the support of American Zionists for the proposal."[7] In April 1936, in his talks with Antonius, he had insisted on the inclusion of Transjordan and the Golan in any Jewish state that would arise in Palestine. Now, however, Ben-Gurion became a fervent advocate of partition, and immediately set to work drafting his own plan, which would serve the Zionists as a basis for negotiation. So thoroughly did Ben-Gurion identify himself with partition that there were many in Mapai who believed it was Ben-Gurion who brought Weizmann around to the idea, Weizmann having hesitated at first to endorse the scheme.

Even before the report's publication, Ben-Gurion learned that it included a provision for the transfer of the Arab population within the Jewish state to the territory of the Arab state. The idea was not new to Zionism, and had been advocated by Israel Zangwill, Jacobson, and Jabotinsky. Ben-Gurion had opposed the notion on moral grounds, for it had always been his claim that "we did not come to dispossess the Arabs of their land." In 1929, when he drew up his federation plan, with its strong resemblance to partition, he rejected the idea of an exchange of population. Once again, the issue proved a moral test of Ben-Gurion's vision of Zionism as a just movement.

He did not respond immediately. To Sharett, Ben-Gurion wrote that "it is hard for me to believe in compulsory transfer, and it is hard for me to believe in voluntary transfer."[8] Would the British really agree to compel the movement of people, and would any Arab agree to move voluntarily? Only on second reading of the report did Ben-Gurion determine that the proposal's "importance exceeds that of the report's other merits, and outweighs all of the report's shortcomings."[9] The idea was this: some 225,000 Arabs lived in the area that would be included within the Jewish state, and they were bound to constitute a problem once partition was effected. The Peel Commission suggested the transfer of these Arabs to the Arab state, with British assistance. In the Galilee's valleys, where Ben-Gurion estimated that some 100,000 Arabs lived, the Peel Commission recommended that "in the last resort the exchange would be compulsory." This was, in fact, an "exchange" in name only, for only 1250 Jews lived in the territory earmarked for the proposed Arab state.

Ben-Gurion emerged from his inner struggle with the conviction that the transfer of the Arab population would be a boon to the proposed Jewish state. "The compulsory transfer of the Arabs from the valleys of the proposed Jewish state," he wrote in his diary, "could give us something which we never had, even when we stood on our own during the days of the First and Second Temples": a Galilee almost free of non-Jews. For the first time in history, there would be "a real Jewish state"—"a contiguous, thickly populated, agricultural bloc." The problem of Hebrew labor would be solved as well. "We are being given an opportunity which we never dared to dream of in our wildest imagination. This is more than a state, government and sovereignty—this is national consolidation in a free homeland."[10]

Yet he carefully measured the expediency of the proposal against the claims of justice. "The more I study the recommendations of the Commission," he added in his diary, "I see above all the terrible difficulty in uprooting, by foreign force, some 100,000 Arabs from villages which they have inhabited for hundreds of years."[11] But again, the voice of expediency spoke. A completely Jewish Galilee would give the Jewish state another advantage: a northern border with Lebanon. "This proximity has tremendous political value, because Lebanon and the Jews are both interested in being neighbors. The Christians of Lebanon could hardly exist without a Jewish state alongside them, and we are also interested in an alliance with Christian Lebanon."[12]

Then the doubts returned. "Would Britain dare to do it" in the face of Arab and Muslim opposition? Would Britain also set aside moral calculations? To this, Ben-Gurion replied that Britain "certainly won't do it if we do not insist upon it, if we do not push with all the force of our influence and conviction. Even our maximum pressure may not suffice. But if because of our weakness, neglect or negligence, the thing is not done, then we will have lost a chance which we never had before, and may never have again." Ben-Gurion's conclusion was unequivocal: "We must uproot from our hearts the assumption that the thing is not possible. It *can* be done." As a first "and perhaps decisive" step, "we must prepare ourselves to carry out" the transfer provision.[13]

Ben-Gurion adduced a final moral argument in a letter to his sixteen-year-old son, Amos. Raised on a strict diet of humanitarian values, the boy would not have understood the claims of expedience. "We have never wanted to dispossess the Arabs," his father explained. "But because Britain is giving them part of the country which had been promised to us, it is only fair that the Arabs in our state be transferred to the Arab portion."[14]

The Zionist Congress, convened in Zurich in July 1937, did not reject the partition plan embraced by the British government earlier in the month. A Jewish state in part of Palestine now seemed inevitable, and Ben-Gurion began to busy himself in all sorts of practical preparations for the government of the new sovereign state.

But it was not long before Arab opposition to partition

plunged the country into a still more serious round of bloodshed. The British were determined to suppress the Arab Revolt, particularly after the assassination of Lewis Andrews, acting district commissioner for the Galilee, and his police escort. Palestinian Arab leaders were arrested and sent into exile; others, among them the Mufti, escaped to neighboring countries. But this did not quell the rebellion, and gradually the country was transformed into an armed camp under martial law. By 1938, almost 20,000 British soldiers were stationed in Palestine, and only by sheer force did they finally put down the Arab Revolt in early 1939.

In the meantime, the British government withdrew its support for the partition plan, a step sanctioned by still another commission sent in 1938 to investigate the practical aspects of partition. The Woodhead Commission reported in October 1938 that "we have been unable to recommend boundaries which will afford a reasonable prospect of the eventual establishment of self-supporting Arab and Jewish states." A policy statement issued by the British government with the Woodhead Commission's report determined that the political and financial difficulties involved in partition were so great as to make such a solution to the problem "impracticable."[15] The partition plan was dead.

But not for Ben-Gurion. Although he may not have been aware that his earlier political work had paved a road to partition, the Peel Commission's report convinced him that the future road to Jewish statehood led inexorably through partition. The commission's plan, like a welder's torch, linked Ben-Gurion's past action with his future purpose. By embracing the partition plan, Ben-Gurion again established his willingness to make certain concessions for peace. But they were very specific concessions. Given Britain's renewed determination to wash its hands of the Mandate for Palestine, Ben-Gurion was prepared to sacrifice territory as long as a sovereign Jewish state would be established on the remnant.

Partition was the only answer to Zionism's crisis; only thus could Palestine provide a refuge for the Jews of Germany and Poland.

"The only reason that we agreed to discuss the partition plan," Ben-Gurion wrote to Sharett in September 1938, "is *mass immigration.* Not in the future, and not according to abstract formula, but large immigration, now."[16] Henceforth, partition was his only program, and on those occasions when he still defended the Mandate, it was only to dissuade the Arabs from the belief that partition was a "Jewish plan."

"Before the publication of the Peel Commission's report, I talked of the need for a double struggle: preservation of the mandate and negotiation over a state"—so Ben-Gurion wrote to Katznelson. But "since then, and now, I see the possibility for the creation of a Jewish state as the greatest opportunity which history has ever given us, and the beginning of our complete redemption."[17]

His "either-or" approach came to serve his argument for partition. Either the Jews would have their own state in one part of Palestine, or they would remain a minority in an Arab state occupying all of Palestine. There were no other possibilities. A week before the Woodhead Commission published its report, Ben-Gurion wrote to his children that "even if the partition plan is annulled, it will reappear again sometime, and then it will be essential to establish a Jewish state in part of the country."[18] After the British government withdrew its support for the idea, Ben-Gurion wrote to Dov Joseph that "as far as I can see, there is no solution other than partition."[19] A state, achieved through partition, was his one and only goal.

In 1933, after Hitler rose to power, Ben-Gurion predicted world war. Such a war would threaten not only the Jews of Europe, but the Yishuv in Palestine. The sense of responsibility that he now felt loosened his tongue, and he began to say things in public that he had kept to himself in the past.

He no longer offered convoluted explanations for Arab violence against Jews. "Almost every Arab" opposed Zionism, "because he is an Arab, because he is a Muslim, because he dislikes foreigners, and because we are hateful to him in every way."[20] The conflict had lasted for thirty years, and was liable "to continue for perhaps hundreds more." This was a "real war," "a war of life or death."[21]

Ben-Gurion also feared a possible alliance between Arab states and those forces in Europe "which want to destroy every trace of Jewry," particularly Nazi Germany. In war, what would Britain's attitude toward the Yishuv be? Where would British armies be positioned? Could Britain defend the Yishuv were the independent Arab states, with their armies and air forces, to join Palestine's Arabs in a war against the Jews, who had no regular army? Ben-Gurion did not discount the possibility of "massacre and destruction." "It took us fifty years to build what we have built, and one sandstorm from the desert can lay waste to everything."[22] This was a veiled reference to Ibn Saud, who had already intervened diplomatically in Palestine, and might one day think to intervene militarily.

The Yishuv, therefore, needed help from the outside, to survive any conflagration and to hold out a hand of salvation to the Jews of Germany and Poland. Where would such help come from? Britain was not what she had been before the European crisis, and the British government had begun to turn away from the Mandate and the Balfour Declaration. The Yishuv could only really rely on itself. But it was still small in comparison with the challenge that a world war could pose. Zionism had utterly failed as a voluntary movement of Jews to Palestine, and its prospects brightened only after Europe's Jews fell victim to the worst sort of oppression. Ben-Gurion told Mapai that "at the moment there is a situation which, from an abstract Zionist perspective, is positive. . . . There is no need to make propaganda for Palestine. The lives which Jews are leading in the Diaspora is the most compelling propaganda." Ben-Gurion's aim was to capture the steam generated by the crisis of European Jewry, to drive the engines of Zionism. "Is it possible," he asked, "to transform the tragedy of Jewry into a positive force?"[23] With the reduction of immigration quotas after 1936, the pressure on Palestine's gates grew still more intense, and Ben-Gurion sought to harness these forces to his new formula of peace through strength.

No longer would Ben-Gurion speak of "nondomination" or cite the benefits Zionism would bring to the Arabs through a federative arrangement. Ben-Gurion was led by circumstances to adopt the language of force. Conflict between Arab and Jew was inescapable, and the Arabs were not interested in the blessing promised by Zionism. Displays of good will and attempts at dialogue would not mitigate that conflict. The Arabs would try over and over again to break the Yishuv by political and military assaults, and only after they had despaired of ever destroying the Zionist enemy would they make peace with a force that they could not break. The Arab war against the Jews was expected and inevitable, not only in the opinion of the Arabs, but in Ben-Gurion's own view.

Once he began to speak of peace through strength, Ben-Gurion's entire outlook was transformed. He now began to talk often of the ways in which the Yishuv could grow mighty. His aims were threefold. The first was to bring about peace. It would be "very naive to think that the Arabs will fix their relationship with us according to an abstract notion of justice. Which people in the world relates to others on this basis?" But Arabs and non-Arabs alike understood the language of facts. "And so, if one wants an understanding with the Arabs . . . a precondition is the creation of great Jewish strength," the sooner the better.[24] The second aim was defense against Arab attacks. And the third aim was to impress Britain with the Yishuv's growing military potential in the hope of earning political consideration. Once the Yishuv was a major force, "it will be able to speak to Britain in a different language."[25]

When the Peel Commission recommended the establishment of a Jewish state in part of Palestine, Ben-Gurion immediately began to consider its military requirements. All of the new state's resources would be mobilized for the absorption of mass immigration, but at the same time, he called for an "across-the-board expansion of our armed forces."[26] By September 1939, the number of Jews authorized by the government to carry arms reached 20,000, and these were supplemented by the Haganah underground. Ben-Gurion thought this a considerable force, the size of which the Jewish people had rarely commanded.[27] Its first task was to defend the Yishuv against an all-Arab attack that might follow the outbreak of world war. In August 1937, at the Zionist Congress, Ben-Gurion drew a grim picture of the possible future. The British army stationed in Palestine might well be moved to another front in a crisis, leaving the Yishuv alone and surrounded by Arab armies, which could rush to aid Arab brethren in Palestine. The Arabs would find in world war a "chance to settle old scores."[28] Only a strong Jewish armed force could deter them.[29] At the same time, such a force could stand firmly at Britain's side if need be, or could threaten to block any British attempt to impose Arab will on the Yishuv. Mass immigration and an army, thus, would be the two channels into which the Yishuv-turned-Jewish-state would direct its energies.

But this mass immigration and military strength would serve still another purpose, at which Ben-Gurion only hinted. Only initiates knew that Ben-Gurion regarded the creation of a Jewish state in part of Palestine as a stage in the longer process toward a Jewish state in all of Palestine. In the small portion of Palestine allotted to the Jewish state by the Peel Commission, it would not be possible to absorb the whole Jewish people, or even most of it. That people was in desperate straits. And so Ben-Gurion spoke in ambiguous tones about a state being but a step toward "a complete solution for the Jewish people and a powerful instrument for the total fulfillment of Zionism, an instrument for the redemption of all the Land of Israel."[30] In a secret report to Mapai, Ben-Gurion wrote that "there is the possibility that a Jewish state will be established soon . . . which will serve as an important and decisive *stage* in the realization of Zionism."[31] In October 1938, he wrote to his children that "I don't regard a state in part of Palestine as the final aim of Zionism, but as a means toward that aim."[32] In September 1937, Ben-Gurion offered some insight into his thought to a group of Jewish labor leaders in New York, when he told them that "the borders [of the Jewish state] will not be fixed for eternity."[33]

In a letter to his son Amos, in October 1937, Ben-Gurion forthrightly embraced territorial expansionism. A Jewish state in part of Palestine was "not the end, but only the beginning." Its establishment would give a "powerful boost to our historic efforts to redeem the country in its entirety." For the Jewish state would have an "outstanding army—I have no doubt that our army will be among the world's outstanding—and so I am certain that we won't be constrained from settling in the rest of the country, either by mutual agreement and understanding with our Arab neighbors, or by some other way."

Ben-Gurion was prepared to fight for the right to settle Jews anywhere in the country. "I still believe . . . that after we become numerous and strong, the Arabs will understand that it is best for them to strike an alliance with us, and to benefit from our help, providing they allow us by their good will to settle in all parts of Palestine."

As an example, Ben-Gurion cited the Negev, which was not included in the Jewish state proposed by the Peel Commission, and which was for the most part empty of inhabitants. "It is very possible that in exchange for our financial, military, organizational and scientific assistance, the Arabs will agree that we develop and build the Negev. It is also possible that they won't agree. No people always behaves according to logic, common sense, and best interests." If the Arabs "act according to sterile nationalist emotion," and reject the idea of Jewish settlement, preferring that the Negev remain barren, then the Jewish army would act. "Because we cannot stand to see large areas of unsettled land capable of absorbing thousands of Jews remain empty, or to see Jews not return to their country because the Arabs say that there is not enough room for them and us."

In reflecting on the transfer provision of the Peel Commission's recommendations, Ben-Gurion planned his next step: "We must expel Arabs and take their places." He did not wish to do so, for "all our aspiration is built on the assumption—proven throughout all our activity—that there is enough room for ourselves and the Arabs in Palestine." But if the Arabs did not accept that assumption, "and if we have to use force—not to dispossess the Arabs of the Negev and Transjordan, but to guarantee our own right to settle in those places—then we have force at our disposal."[34]

Ben-Gurion did not think that the Arabs of Palestine would fight alone in this battle. "It is very possible that the Arabs of neighboring countries will come to their aid against us. But our strength will exceed theirs. Not only because we will be better organized and equipped, but because behind us there stands a still larger force, superior in quantity and quality." For it was clear to Ben-Gurion that "the whole younger generation" of Jews, in Europe and America, "will rush to join us in the event of such a conflict—which I pray will never occur."[35]

On his return to Palestine that same month, Ben-Gurion convened Mapai activists in Tel Aviv and delivered a lecture on future prospects. He divided the realization of "the historic aim of the Jewish state" into two stages. The first stage, which would last ten or fifteen years, he called "the period of building and laying foundations." This would prepare the state for the second stage, "the period of expansion." The goal of both stages was the "gathering in of the exiles in all of Palestine." And so "from the moment the state is established, it must calculate its actions with an eye toward this distant goal." The concept of peace through strength thus added two new principles to Ben-Gurion's doctrine. Unlike in the past, when he spoke of the division of the country along national lines, Ben-Gurion now aspired to achieve a "*Jewish* Palestine."[36] And whereas in the past, he had spoken of "conquering" the land through cultivation of barren wasteland and feverish work, Ben-Gurion now assigned a role to armed force. The state in the making would be Jewish and expansionist.

The world had come on hard times, and they were still harder for the Jews, in Europe and Palestine. In March 1938, Nazi armies invaded Austria, which Hitler then annexed to Germany. He then began to press his claim to the Sudetenland. Western alliances and promises proved worthless. The breakdown of the European order "will make a profound impression upon the Arab world," Ben-Gurion thought, and "the work of Hitler's and Mussolini's agents in the Near East" would be made easier. If war broke out, "the Arab and Muslim world is liable to rise in revolt . . . and the British Empire will be in danger." And so Britain could be expected to try harder than ever before to appease the Arabs and earn their sympathy.

In September 1938, Neville Chamberlain and Adolf Hitler signed the Munich Agreement, and in October, only a few days after his return from Munich, Chamberlain sealed the fate of the partition plan and the proposed Jewish state. The chance for Jewish independence and Czech freedom were signed away by the same British government, ending all hope for peace in Europe and the salvation of Europe's Jewry through a state in Palestine.

Ben-Gurion now saw a world in which force, not justice,

prevailed. His vision of Zionism, too, underwent a transformation. He had once viewed Zionism as absolutely just; now necessity demanded that he lower his moral sights. In April 1936, Ben-Gurion concluded that no people on earth determined its relations with other peoples by abstract moral calculations of justice. "There is only one thing that everyone accepts, Arabs and non-Arabs alike: *facts*."[37] The Arabs would not make peace with the Jews "out of sentiment for justice," but because such a peace at some point would become worthwhile and advantageous. A Jewish state would encourage peace, because with it the Jews would "become a force, and the Arabs respect force."[38] Ben-Gurion explained to Mapai that "these days it is not right but might which prevails. It is more important to have force than justice on one's side." In a period of "power politics, the powers that be become hard of hearing, and respond only to the roar of cannons. And the Jews in the Diaispora have no cannons."[39] In order to survive in this evil world, the Jewish people needed cannons more than justice.

Britain was now determined to placate the Arabs and win their sympathy, as well as the sympathy of Muslims throughout the world. To do so, the British government wished to turn troublesome Palestine over to its inhabitants, seventy percent of whom were Arabs in 1938. Even before this retreat from the Mandate became official British policy, Ben-Gurion anticipated the sea change. The Zionist response, now that the idea of a Jewish state had been spurned by Britain, was to insist that Britain continue to administer the Mandate for Palestine. But the odds were heavily stacked against this campaign, for as Colonial Secretary Malcolm MacDonald told Weizmann, there could be no "return to the mandate."[40] Instead, Britain would take an active role in "bringing about an agreement between Jews and Arabs,"[41] and if such an agreement could not be reached, then a solution would be imposed.

Ben-Gurion dreaded either possibility, for he knew that Britain's mind had already been made up. "The situation is more or less clear: the government has decided to hand us over to the Arabs. No state and no immigration."[42] To carry this policy through, Britain called for a round table conference of all the parties to the dispute, to find a quick and long-term solution to the problems of Palestine. Then, if Jews and Arabs failed to reach an accommodation, Britain would have a license to impose its own solution. Ben-Gurion regarded the proposed conference as a British ploy to push through a policy fixed in advance. "I don't see any chance for this negotiation. I think we will lose tooth and eye, and afterwards the Mandate will be abolished—of this I am almost certain."[43] Independence for Palestine, now, meant an Arab state, "because the Arabs are more than a two-thirds majority."[44]

The conference met at St. James Palace during February and March 1939. Because the Arabs refused to sit at the same negotiating table with the Jews, the talks were held through British intermediaries, while both delegations sat in separate rooms under the same roof. Britain's self-appointed role as the honest broker did not have a moderating effect, and the Jews freely expressed their view that the talks were bound to fail. The Arabs reiterated their unchanging demands: the establishment of an independent Arab state in Palestine with a guaranteed Arab majority. It soon became clear that this was British policy as well, and the Zionists withdrew from the talks. The conference thus collapsed.

But the experience was important for Ben-Gurion. He did meet, informally, a number of Arab leaders and personalities before and during the negotiations, in minor talks. These Arabs, however, were not from Palestine but from neighboring states. The Palestinian Arab participants in the conference avoided all such contact, and so Ben-Gurion's talks with these other Arabs were essentially tactical maneuvers, and yielded nothing. Ben-Gurion's meetings with George Antonius in 1936 remained his last direct contact with an Arab figure from Palestine. In any case, Ben-Gurion was already convinced that Palestine's Arabs would come around to an agreement only after they had despaired of defeating the Yishuv, and so he anticipated war. For Ben-Gurion, the Yishuv's relationship with the Arabs of Palestine was now a military and not a political question.

This preparedness for war came across dramatically in an exchange with Colonial Secretary MacDonald, as reported by Ben-Gurion. MacDonald asked: "How much longer do you think we will put our bayonets at the disposal of Jewish immigration?" Ben-Gurion replied: "Fine, as you wish. Withdraw your bayonets. Immigration doesn't need your bayonets. Quite the opposite. Only British bayonets can prevent the immigration of Jews. All that we ask is that you don't use your bayonets against immigration." MacDonald replied: "And defense? Who will defend you? Don't you need our bayonets for the security of the Yishuv?" Ben-Gurion's response: "We can do without your bayonets to defend the Yishuv. Let us defend ourselves. Don't stand in our way." MacDonald: "How is that possible? They're double your numbers." Ben-Gurion: "That's our problem." MacDonald: "Not just double. They will bring reinforcement from Iraq, an Arab army." Ben-Gurion: "Never mind, we'll also bring in reinforcement. It is easier to cross the sea than the desert. . . . We inform you that we no longer need your bayonets, not for immigration, and not for our security. . . . Our immigration and our Yishuv can stand on their own, with the help of the Jewish people."[45] Even at hope's nadir, when a Jewish state seemed impossible, Ben-Gurion was certain of the Yishuv's strength and was prepared to rely on it.

In May 1939, the Chamberlain government issued a White Paper, which spelled out in detail the solution Great Britain intended to impose. In ten year's time, Palestine would become an independent state. Two five-year transitional periods would precede this independence. During these periods, representatives of the various communities would draw up a constitution, which would guarantee, among other things, the status of the Jewish minority. At the same time, 75,000 Jews would be allowed to enter Palestine, so that the Jews might constitute exactly one third of the country's population. All subsequent Jewish immigration would be subject to Arab approval. Jewish land purchases would also be narrowly restricted to parts of the country populated predominantly by Jews.

As far as Ben-Gurion was concerned, the White Paper was but one more chapter in the saga of surrender by Great Britain to "violent forces."[46] "The White Paper is nothing but a new edition of Munich." So often did he repeat this charge that it became embedded in Zionist consciousness. At Munich, a small people, the Czechs, were surrendered to Hitler. In the White Paper, the Jews, "a helpless and hopeless people," were turned over to the Mufti and his terrorist gangs.[47] Great Britain had not only abandoned a commitment to promote immigration but had assumed a new obligation, "to *prevent* immigration by *force*."[48] The Jews, Ben-Gurion concluded, had no alternative but to struggle to reopen the gates and to defeat the White Paper.

A wave of protest demonstrations swept Palestine, as the Yishuv vented its anger against the harsh decree. This was the beginning of the long war against the White Paper, which was to culiminate in the establishment of the State of Israel. This was also Ben-Gurion's finest hour. Not only did he stand at the forefront of what he called "fighting Zionism,"[49] but he lent the struggle the distinctive stamp of his personality. For it was Ben-Gurion who had to explain exactly how to defeat the White Paper, and in doing so, he seized the Yishuv's imagination.

At first, he simply said that this was not a war against Great Britain and the British people. It was directed against only one British policy, a policy that was not essential to Great Britain's wider security and about which the British themselves were of a divided opinion. "War against the policy of liquidating the Mandate—from a pro-British orientation."[50] With the invasion of Poland and the entry of Great Britain into the European war, the need became apparent for a clearer explanation of the seeming contradiction.

In attempting to answer to that need, Ben-Gurion coined the most memorable of his couplets. "No war against England and the English," he declared in September 1939, "but war against the policy of the British government."[51] But this formula was still too abstract and ambiguous. Four days later, genius touched him: "We must assist the British army as though there were no White Paper; and we must oppose the White Paper as though there were no world war."[52] This slogan became corrupted as it passed from mouth to mouth, until it took this final form: war against Hitler as though there were no White Paper; war against the White Paper as though there were no Hitler.

Both of these wars were intended to strengthen the Yishuv, to make it a power of consequence. In aiding the British war effort, the Yishuv's own military capabilities were greatly expanded. Jews were trained by the British in the military arts, and the Yishuv's industries tooled up for wartime production. Ben-Gurion directed this mobilization of the Yishuv for British war ends, out of the conviction that the Jews would emerge hardened for their own contest with the Arabs. The other war, against the White Paper, would also bolster the Yishuv. The suffering and desperation of European Jewry constituted a "tremendous force, of inestimable value." These Jews would arrive in their millions at the gates of Palestine, and Great Britain would be powerless to stop the movement, for "a British government which needs to fire on Jewish ships will not last a week."[53] But this war never took on the dimensions anticipated by Ben-Gurion. The Jews of Europe, quite simply, did not arrive. Hitler planned another fate for them. There were few ships, and no need to fire on them.

The tragedy of European Jewry did eventually strengthen the Yishuv, in an unexpected way. In August 1937, Ben-Gurion already noted that "Jewish suffering is also a political factor," and "whoever says that Hitler diminished our strength, is not telling the whole truth."[54] In one of history's crueler ironies, those words proved prophetic. Millions of Jews did not storm the beaches of Palestine, for they could not rise from the ashes of the death camps. But the Holocaust—the zenith of Jewish agony—became the same "political force" of which Ben-Gurion spoke before he even imagined the systematic destruction of European Jewry. After the war, the Holocaust was a powerfully influential factor in turning world public opinion in Zionism's favor, and was the decisive factor in defeating the policy of the White Paper. Guilt, sorrow, and remorse—what might be called the collective conscience of humanity—led many nations finally to grant the survivors, that which might have saved the many victims: a Jewish state in the Land of Israel.

Epilogue

In April 1939, following the St. James Conference, Ben-Gurion informed Mapai that "in this terrible and mad hour, . . . there is not a single political leader among the Arabs, both in Palestine and in neighboring countries, who is prepared to talk with us about an agreement in which the Jews would not remain a minority for eternity. We won't take part in such a discussion."[1] Ben-Gurion now accepted the conflict between Arab and Jewish aspirations as an unalterable fact. Only the use of force could bring about a change. In 1966, Ben-Gurion described his talks with Arab leaders as "a failed attempt," and this was the title that he briefly considered for his book later published as *My Talks with Arab Leaders*. His remarks to Mapai thus represented his summary of the past, and his prognosis for the future.

Ben-Gurion could trace his view back to his very first years in Palestine, and he often did so. His well-known story about his 1915 encounter with his fellow law student, Yahya Effendi, in Jerusalem's jail, took on apocryphal significance. Yahya, on learning that Ben-Gurion was to be expelled from the country, told him that "as your friend, I am sorry. As an Arab, I rejoice." In a letter to Justice Louis Brandeis in 1940,

Ben-Gurion repeated this story, and added that "from my experience in Palestine, this is also the true attitude of even the best Arabs." "One must distinguish between the Arab as an individual, and as a member of a political community," Ben-Gurion concluded.[2] In short, all the Arabs were Yahya Effendis.

To remove all doubt, Ben-Gurion went still further. Arabs who supported terror, and those who opposed it, were nonetheless united politically in their adherence to two principles: an end to Jewish immigration, and full independence for Arab Palestine. Furthermore, "the Arab is a political creature who is unable to withstand the pressures of his environment, or the emotive and collective drives of his people." In all of Palestine, Ben-Gurion did not know of a single Arab of political significance who would consent to continued immigration or a Palestine in which Jews were anything but a minority. A political settlement was impossible; all that was thinkable was some measure of economic cooperation. But this cooperation, he wrote to Brandeis, "will not lead to a political accord."[3]

Ben-Gurion's claim that he knew of Arab opposition to Zionism as early as 1915 raises serious questions about the sincerity of his professed positions on the "Arab question." In fact, as early as 1910, Ben-Gurion recognized that a conflict existed between Arab and Jewish aspirations, and later in 1914 he asked, concerning the Arabs, "Who hates us as they do?" In 1916, he openly spoke and wrote about the "hatred" of the Arabs for the Jews in Palestine. Only in the years between 1917 and 1936 did he avoid mention of the conflict and even denied its existence.

But this was his public position. In his diary, and behind the closed doors of party fora, he showed himself alert to the problem of Arab rejection. A careful comparison of Ben-Gurion's public and private positions leads inexorably to the conclusion that this twenty-year denial of the conflict was a calculated tactic, born of pragmatism rather than profundity of conviction. The idea that Jews and Arabs could reconcile their differences through class solidarity, a notion he championed between 1919 and 1929, was a delaying tactic. Once the Yishuv had gained strength, Ben-Gurion abandoned it. The belief in a compromise solution, which Ben-Gurion professed for the seven years between 1929 and 1936, was also a tactic, designed to win continued British support for Zionism. The only genuine convictions that underlay Ben-Gurion's approach to the Arab question were two: that the support of the power that ruled Palestine was more important to Zionism than any agreement with the Arabs, and that the Arabs would reconcile themselves to the Jewish presence only after they conceded their inability to destroy it.

With the publication of the White Paper in May 1939, reliance on the power that ruled Palestine became impractical, for Great Britain now stood opposed to Zionism. Ben-Gurion still hoped to change the direction of British policy. But until then, Zionism required a policy based on force, to counter force and the threat of force. Given the provisions of the White Paper, peace was no longer a "fundamental requirement" of Zionism. As long as the British had supported Zionism, "we had a need, I wouldn't say for mutual love, but for peace with the Arabs." This would make the British task of promoting Zionism easier.

But the 1939 White Paper, in directing British policy toward the establishment of Palestine as an Arab state, made a basic reassessment unavoidable. "Peace is no longer our fundamental requirement," Ben-Gurion now averred. "Peace in Palestine is not the best situation for thwarting the policy of the White Paper." Nor, for that matter, did economic cooperation with the Arabs seem worthwhile, as long as a political settlement remained remote. There was no point now in "simply doing favors for the Arabs." The idea of Zionism selflessly aiding the Arabs—"that we must show concern for the Arabs"—Ben-Gurion termed "moral corruption."[4] In doing so, he set aside his vision of Zionism as a peace-seeking movement, desirous of bettering the Arab condition. It would not be long before Ben-Gurion would prepare not for peace but for war, a war made inevitable after the Biltmore Plan of 1942 declared Zionism's explicit aim to be a Jewish state, which the Arabs were determined to oppose by force.

As at St. James, so throughout the war years, the Zionists and the Arabs of Palestine did not meet and talk. The Arab Bureau of the Jewish Agency did maintain a fairly wide, informal network of contacts with Arabs, more often with those from neighboring countries than from Palestine. But the personnel of the Bureau knew that Ben-Gurion believed peace had no chance, and their activities remained confined to the gathering of information and maneuvers to split Arab ranks.

Ben-Gurion, in the meantime, busied himself in preparations for war. Through his campaign to mobilize the Yishuv in support of the British war effort, he strove to build the nucleus of a "Hebrew army," and his success in this endeavor later brought victory to Zionism in the struggle to establish a Jewish state. At the same time, Ben-Gurion turned his eyes again to a world power, the United States, in his quest for a prop to replace Great Britain. As early as 1940, he predicted American ascendance as a great world power, and his cultivating of American public and official opinion yielded fruit. Without a United States sympathetic to Zionism, it is doubtful the United Nations would have voted, on November 29, 1947, for the partition of Palestine into Jewish and Arab states.

The Arabs of Palestine—with the support of Arab states—rejected the partition plan of the United Nations and did not establish their own state. The Jews did otherwise. On May 15, 1948, Ben-Gurion proclaimed the establishment of the State of Israel. The Arabs, as he expected, declared war. The Arabs of Palestine rose up against Israel, and the armies of Egypt, Jordan, Iraq, and Syria, invaded her territory. In this year-long contest, in which much blood was shed, Israel emerged triumphant, as Ben-Gurion had predicted in 1937.

The fate of Palestine's Arabs was now sealed. Some became citizens of Israel. Some became citizens of Jordan, which annexed the West Bank. Others became second-class citizens of Egypt, which occupied the Gaza Strip. Still others became refugees in other Arab countries. And so the Arab question was dropped from the Zionist agenda, to be replaced by the question of Israel's security. After 1948, the matter of the Palestinian Arabs became bound up in the wars between Israel and its neighboring Arab states. So began a new and distinct chapter in the history of both peoples.

Notes

Abbreviations in the Notes

Archives

BB	Israel Labor Party Archives, Kfar Saba (Beit Berl)
CAHJP	The Central Archives for the History of the Jewish People (Toldot Ha-Am he-Yehudi), Jerusalem
CZA	The Central Zionist Archives, Jerusalem
FO	Archives of the Foreign Office, Public Records Office, London
HE	Archives of the Executive Committee of the Histadrut, Tel Aviv
IDF	Military (IDF) and Defense Establishment Archives, Givatayim
L	Archives and Museum of the Israel Labor Movement, Tel Aviv
MBG	The Ben-Gurion Archives, Sde Boqer Campus. (Includes all diaries and letters of DBG that are not attributed in notes to any other archival collection.)
WA	The Weizmann Archives, Rehovot

Protocols

HISC	Protocols of the Histadrut Conventions & Councils, located in Archives and Museum of the Israel Labor Movement, Tel Aviv
HISE	Protocols of the Histadrut Executive Committee, located in the Archives of the Executive Committee of the Histadrut, Tel Aviv
JAG	Protocols of the Jewish Agency Directorate, in the Central Zionist Archives, Jerusalem
MAP	Protocols of Mapai, in Israel Labor Party Archives, Kfar Saba (Beit Berl)

ZER Protocols of the smaller Zionisdt Actions Committee, located in the Central Zionist Archives, Jerusalem

DBG's Memoirs, Speeches, and Articles

AS *Anahnu ve-Shkheneinu (We and Our Neighbors)*. Tel Aviv: Davar Publishing, 5691 (1931)

IG *Igrot (Letters)*. Tel Aviv: Am Oved and Tel Aviv University. In three volumes, 1971–1974

MLA *Mi-Ma'amad le-Am (From Class to Peoplehood)*. Tel Aviv: Davar Publishing, 5693 (1933)

MP *Michtavim el Paula ve-el ha-Yeladim (Letters to Paula and the Children)*. Tel Aviv: Am Oved, 5728 (1968)

PMA *Pegishotai im Manhigim Araviyim (My Meetings with Arab Leaders)*. Tel Aviv: Am Oved, 1967

YBG *Yoman (Diary)*. (Loose documents, not an edited collection)

ZBG *Zikhronot (Memoirs)*. Tel Aviv: Am Oved. In 5 volumes, 1971–1982

Other Memoirs and Collections

BK Berl Katznelson. *Kitvei Berl Katznelson (The Writings of Berl Katznelson)*. Mapai Publishing. In 12 volumes

DV Itzhak Tabenkin. *Dvarim (Papers)*. Ha-Kibbutz Ha-Me'uhad Publishing. In 7 volumes, 1967–1981

Secondary Works

KD Shabtai Teveth. *Kin'at David (David's Jealousy)*. Jerusalem: Schoken, 1977, 1980. In 2 volumes

STH Ben-Zion Dinur et al. ed. *Sefer Toldot Ha-Haganah (History of the Haganah)*. Tel Aviv: Ma'arachot Publishing. In 4 volumes, 1964

Notes to Preface

1. DBG's Introduction to *AS*, dated May 27, 1931.
2. *MAP* (Council) October 15, 1930.

Notes to Chapter 1

1. *KD*, vol. I, pp. 11–21.
2. DBG's remarks to Mapai section of Twentieth Zionist Congress, August 18, 1939, *IDF* 2957.

3. *Ma'arekhet Sinai*, Tel Aviv. Am Oved, 1964, p. 130.
4. *AS*, pp. 104, 148.
5. *IG*, vol. I, p. 71.
6. Ibid., p. 75.
7. *KD*, vol. I, p. 87.
8. *AS*, p. 9.
9. *KD*, vol. I, pp. 94, 96.
10. Ibid., p. 99.
11. Ibid., p. 101.
12. Ibid., p. 107.
13. Ibid., p. 130.
14. DBG's article in *Davar*, July 16, 1971; *KD*, vol. I, p. 149.
15. *KD*, vol. I, p. 121.
16. *IG*, vol. I, p. 118.
17. *KD*, vol. I, p. 141.
18. Ibid., pp. 152–154.
19. Ibid., p. 158.
20. DBG's letter to Paula from London, June 3, 1939, *MBG*.
21. *ZBG*, vol. II, p. 49.
22. DBG's lecture as published in *Ha'ahdut*, no. 3, Eylul 5670 (1910), and nos. 2 and 3, Tishrei 5671 (1910).
23. *AS*, pp. 273, 276.
24. *Forward* (Yiddish), June 3, 1916; *KD*, vol. I, p. 345.
25. *KD*, vol. I, p. 345.
26. Report on the Third Conference in Vienna, *Ha'ahdut*, vol. 2, no. 43, 5671 (1910–1911).
27. A. Reuveni, *Ad Yerushalayim*, Tel Aviv, 5714 (1953–1954), pp. 42–45.
28. *Ha'ahdut*, no. 3, Elul 5670 (1910).
29. Ibid.

Notes to Chapter 2

1. *Ha'ahdut*, no. 1, Tammuz 5670 (1910); *KD*, vol. I, p. 163.
2. *Ha'ahdut*, nos. 2 and 3, Tishrei 5671 (1910); *KD*, vol. I, p. 177.
3. Ibid.
4. ZBG, vol. I, p. 52.
5. Report from the World Conference of Poalei Zion, in *Ha'ahdut*, nos. 44, 45, and 46, 5673 (1912–1913).
6. *KD*, vol. I, p. 251.
7. Ibid., p. 275.

8. ZBG, vol. I, p. 71.
9. Ibid.; *KD*, vol. I, pp. 288f.
10. "Towards the Future," published in *Hatoren*, no. 5, 5675 (1914–1915); *AS*, p. 1.
11. Omaha notes in CZA, A116/40/1.
12. *Eretz Israel be-Avar uva-Hoveh*. Jerusalem: Ben-Zvi Institute, 5740 (1979–1980).
13. *AS*, p. 55.

Notes to Chapter 3

1. "Upon England's Declaration," *Yiddisher Kemfer* no. 41, November 14, 1917; *MLA*, p. 14.
2. *Hatoren*, vol. 4, nos. 49–50; *AS*, p. 35; *Eretz Israel be-Avar*, pp. 44f.
3. "Towards the Future," *Hatoren*, no. 5, 5675 (1914–1915).
4. "The Fulfillment of Zionism," *Yiddisher Kemfer* no. 41, November 17, 1917; *MLA*, p. 15.
5. "Towards the Future."
6. *AS*, p. 151.
7. Ibid., p. 98.
8. Ibid., p. 31. The item was first published in the *Yiddisher Kemfer*, no. 4, January 22, 1918.
9. *AS*, p. 151.
10. Ibid., p. 33.
11. Speech to railworkers, Haifa, *Ha'aretz*, January 19, 1925; *AS*, p. 77.
12. *AS*, p. 151.
13. Ibid., p. 259.
14. "From the Debate," a dialogue with members of Brith Shalom, November 10, 1929; *AS*, p. 184.
15. *AS*, p. 33.
16. Ibid., p. 98.
17. *KD*, vol. II, pp. 90–103, for an account of the Comintern affair.
18. *AS*, p. 61.
19. "Two Factors," speech at the Fourteenth Zionist Congress, *AS*, p. 97.
20. "A Reply to Ahmed Hamdi," *AS*, p. 138.
21. *MLA*, p. 15.
22. *AS*, p. 33.
23. Ibid., pp. 54–55.
24. "The Dangers of Capitalism," *Yiddisher Kemfer* March 22, 1918, republished in *MLA*, p. 26.
25. Ibid.

26. *AS*, pp. 55–56.
27. Speech before railworkers, *Ha'aretz*, January 19, 1925, republished in *AS*, p. 76.
28. *AS*, p. 69.
29. Ibid., p. 64.
30. *PMA*, p. 10.

Notes to Chapter 4

1. *Yalkut Ahdut Ha'avodah*, vol. I, p. 200.
2. Ibid., p. 209. On the denial see Neil Caplan, *Palestine Jewry and the Arab Question* 1917–1925, London, Cass, 1978.
3. Ibid., p. 214.
4. Ibid., p. 212.
5. Berl Katznelson, "Yizkor," *Yalkut Ahdut Ha'avodah*, vol. I, p. 211.
6. *Yalkut Ahdut Ha'avodah*, vol. I, p. 220.
7. "The 'Demonstration' in Jaffa," *Yalkut Ahdut Ha'avodah*, vol. I, p. 218.
8. Storrs letter of March 1919 and Clayton telegram of March 26, 1919, *F0371/4253*.
9. *Hapoel Hatzair*, no. 26, April 12, 1920.
10. Berl Katznelson, "Jerusalem Days," *Yalkut Ahdut Ha'avodah*, vol. I, p. 230.
11. Itzhak Tabenkin, "Time to Act," *Yalkut Ahdut Ha'avodah*, vol. I, p. 237.
12. A point established decisively by Elie Kedourie in his *Chatham House Version and Other Middle-Eastern Studies*. London, Weidenfeld and Nicholson, 1970, p. 57.
13. Ahdut Ha'avodah protocols for April 20, May 21, May 25, 1920, *L*, 404IV.
14. Cache of letters and telegrams, *IDF* 4019.
15. *Daily Herald*, April 9, 1920; *KD*, vol. II, p. 63.
16. "We Accuse," *Yalkut Ahdut Ha'avodah*, vol. I, p. 221.
17. *IG*, vol. II, pp. 76, 80.
18. *Kunteres*, 10 Heshvan 5682 (November 11, 1921). The following quotes are taken from this source.
19. Jabotinsky, "On the Iron Wall," in *Ze'ev Jabotinsky, Ha-Ish u-Mishnato*. Tel Aviv, Ministry of Defense, 1980, p. 233.
20. *MLA*, p. 4.
21. DBG's remarks to Jewish Agency, *JAG*.
22. "Relations with Our Neighbors," *AS*, p. 61.

Notes to Chapter 5

1. *HISE*, December 20, 1920; October 28, 1921.
2. Sh. Ben-Zvi, "On the Proposal by Comrade Ben-Gurion," *Kunteres*, no. 93.
3. DBG, "On the Agenda for the Histadrut Council," *Kunteres*, no. 106.
4. Decision of the Histadrut Council, January 28–30, 1922, *L; ZBG*, vol. I, p. 210.
5. Account of the Fourth Conference of the Railworkers' Union, *Kunteres*, no. 114; *ZBG*, vol. I, p. 210.
6. Letter from the Executive to the Railworkers' Union, November 23, 1923, *IDF* 2453.
7. *Protocol ha-Ve'ida ha-Shniya shel ha-Histadrut Ha-Clallit, 5683/1923*, ed. Mordechai Sever, 1968, p. 30; *AS*, p. 66.
8. *Protocol*, p. 94.
9. *Din ve-Heshbon le-Ve'ida ha-Shlishit shel ha-Histadrut, Tammuz 5687*(1927), p. 64.
10. "From the Railway Workers' Council," *Kunteres*, no. 165.
11. Ibid.; *AS*, p. 67.
12. *AS*, p. 71.
13. Ibid., p. 63.
14. *Kunteres*, no. 172; *Sefer ha-Ve'ida ha-Revi'it shel Ahdut Ha'avodah; Yalkut Ahdut Ha'avodah*, vol. I, p. 291.
15. *Ibid.; ibid.; ibid.; AS*, p. 72.
16. *Kunteres*, no. 173; *Sefer ha-Ve'ida ha-Revi'it; Yalkut Ahdut Ha'avodah*, vol. I, p. 291; *BK*, vol. II, p. 101.
17. Ibid.; ibid.; ibid.; *DV*, vol. I, p. 352.
18. Zalman Aran, *Autobiografia*. Tel Aviv, Am Oved 1971, p. 177.
19. *AS*, p. 158.
20. DBG's ideas on autonomy can be found in *Sefer ha-Ve'ida ha-Revi'it*, pp. 138ff.; and in a lecture delivered on December 21, 1929, *CZA*, J1/8766II; see also *KD*, vol. II, p. 55; and above all, DBG's "To the Establishment of National Autonomy," *Kunteres*, no. 168.
21. Article by Kaplansky in *Kunteres*, 327.
22. *Kunteres*, no. 172; *Sefer ha-Ve'ida ha-Revi'it; AS*, p. 72; *BK*, vol. II, p. 101.
23. DBG's lecture, *Davar*, January 14, 1926; *AS*, p. 110.

Notes to Chapter 6

1. DBG's speech, October 16, 1928, *CZA*, J1/7232; *Davar*, October 19, 1928; *AS*, p. 156.

2. *YBG*, August 25, 1929.
3. Ibid.; *ZBG*, vol. I, p. 362.
4. Cable from DBG at sea, *ZBG*, vol. I, p. 362.
5. DBG's response to the violence, before Zionist Executive and Va'ad Le'umi, in *CZA*, J1/7232; Ahdut Ha'avodah manifesto, September 19, 1929, *Kunteres*, no. 380; *AS*, p. 160; 23rd Histadrut Council, September 25–26, 1929, *HISC*.
6. *HISE*, September 5, 1929.
7. *HISE*, September 5, October 27, 1929.
8. Ahdut Ha'avodah manifesto (see note 5).
9. Ibid.
10. *YBG*, July 13, 1922.
11. Third Conference of Ahdut Ha'avodah, December 10–17, 1922, *Kunteres*, no. 119.
12. Manifesto of Ahdut Ha'avodah and Hapoel Hatzair, *Kunteres*, no. 380, September 19, 1929; republished in *AS*, p. 160.
13. "Clarifications," in *AS*, p. 179.
14. The memorandum that included the plan for fortifying the Yishuv is preserved in *L* 208, IV, file 225, and in *IDF* 794. See also *ZBG*, vol. I, pp. 362 and 365.
15. *HISE*, September 5, 1929.
16. Memorandum cited in note 14.

Notes to Chapter 7

1. Lecture by DBG in his home in Tel Aviv, November 9, 1929, *IDF* 2036.
2. Memorandum on the security of the Yishuv, September 23, 1929, *WA; ZBG*, vol. I, p. 362.
3. Founding conference of Mapai, *MAP*, January 6, 1930.
4. *HISE*, September 5, 1929.
5. Session of the Va'ad Le'umi, September 8, 1929, *CZA*, J1/7232.
6. Memorandum to the Socialist International from Ahdut Ha'avodah, "On the Arab Riots over the Western Wall," *ZBG*, vol. 1, appendices, pp. 740–750.
7. *KD*, vol. I, pp. 127, 135, and 433.
8. *YBG*, November 8, 1929.
9. Ibid., November 2–5, 1929.
10. Ibid., November 3, 1929.
11. Ibid., November 5, 1929.
12. Ibid., November 6, 1929.

13. Ibid., November 7, 1929.
14. Ibid., November 8–9, 1929.
15. DBG's lecture in his home, November 9, 1929, *IDF* 2036.
16. Letter of invitation to DBG of November 22, 1925, *L* 104IV/DBG.
17. *YBG*, November 30, 1925; *AS*, pp. 81–83.
18. Arthur Ruppin, *Pirkei Hayyai*, vol. III, p. 178; *AS*, pp. 182–87.
19. "Premises," *AS*, p. 188. The following quotes were taken from this source.
20. "Palestina im Rahmen des Nahen Orient," *Zionistische Handbuch*. Berlin, 1923.
21. DBG's speech to founding conference of Mapai, January 6, 1930, *Hapoel Hatzair*, May 22, 1930; and DBG's remarks to Mapai Council, March 21–24, 934, *MAP* and *IDF* 1393.
22. Notes in DBG's handwriting, October 25–27, 1929; Zalman Aran files, *BB*, section 2, no. 22/2.
23. DBG's lecture in his home, November 9, 1929, *IDF* 2036.
24. Ibid.
25. *AS*, p. 188.

Notes to Chapter 8

1. Z. Aran Diary, December 1, 1929, *BB*, section 2, no. 22/2.
2. *YBG*, November 9, 1936; *MAP*, November 9, 1936.
3. Aran Diary, December 1, 1929.
4. Ibid., December 14, 1929.
5. Ibid., December 17, 1929.
6. Text of DBG's lecture on the "Tasks of the United Party," January 6, 1930, *L* 1/405IV.
7. Letter form Moshe Beilinson to Berl Katznelson, January 15, 1930, *BB*.
8. Aran Diary, January 6, 1930.
9. Letter from Beilinson to Katznelson (see note 7 above).
10. Mapai Central Committee, January 9, 1930, *MAP*.
11. Aran Diary, January 9, 1930.
12. Letter from Beilinson to Katznelson (see note 7 above).
13. Report of Shaw Commission (Cmd. 3530).
14. Aran Diary, April 1, 1930.
15. Mapai Secretariat, May 15, 1930, *MAP*.
16. DBG's speech in Haifa, May 20, 1930, *HISE*.
17. Hebrew transcript of meeting with Hope-Simpson, June 4, 1930, *IDF* 2295; *ZBG*, vol. I, p. 395.

18. *YBG*, June 23, 1930; *ZBG*, vol. I, p. 403.
19. *YBG*, June 24, 1930.
20. Opening speech by DBG in Berlin, *Davar*, October 12, 1930.
21. Letter from DBG to Z. Aran, *YBG*, July 10, 1930.
22. DBG in Mapai Central Committee, April 4, 1938, MAP.
23. Summary of DBG's speech to Empire Labor Conference, *YBG*, August 4, 1930; *IG*, vol. III, letter dated July 28, 1930.
24. *ZBG*, vol. I, p. 420; *IG*, vol. III, p. 518.
25. Report of Sir John Hope-Simpson (Cmd. 3686).
26. Mapai Council, October 25, 1930, *MAP*.
27. Ibid.
28. H. Arlosorov, *Yoman Yerushalayim*, Tel Aviv, Mapai, 1953, p. 341.
29. Summary of the debate drawn from the protocol of Mapai Council, February 5–8, 1931, *MAP*.
30. Ibid.
31. Decisions of Mapai Council, February 5–8, 1931, *Hapoel Hatzair*, February 27, 1931.
32. *YBG*, May 17 and June 12, 1931.
33. Introduction to *AS*.

Notes to Chapter 9

1. Akiva Guvrin to the author, February 19, 1974.
2. *YBG*, July 18, 1929.
3. Ibid., October 18, 1925.
4. *Din ve-Heshbon la-Ve'ida ha-Shlishit shel ha-Histadrut*, p. 157.
5. Ibid.
6. Protocol of Histadrut Council, January 7–10, 1929, HISC.
7. Mapai Central Committee, October 2, 1931, *MAP*.
8. Investigation into the matter of an Arabic newspaper, protocol in *L* 208IV, file 214.
9. Ibid.
10. Ibid.
11. *PMA*, p. 18.
12. Ibid.
13. Speech by DBG in the general debate, January 14, 1934; see also *ZBG*, vol. II, p. 11; *PMA*, p. 18.
14. *YBG*, April 10, 1931.
15. Meeting of Mapai Central Committee, November 4, 1933, *MAP; ZBG*, vol. I, p. 685.

16. DBG's letter to Jewish Agency, November 2, 1933; *ZBG*, vol. I, p. 683.
17. Mapai Central Committee (see note 15); DBG letter (see note 16).
18. DBG's letter to Weizmann, October 26, 1933; *IG*, vol. III, p. 360.
19. Protocol of the Zionist Executive Committee, March 29, 1934, typescript, pp. 135–136, *JAG*.

Notes to Chapter 10

1. *PMA*, p. 19.
2. *JAG*, August 9, 1934.
3. *PMA*, p. 19.
4. DBG's letter to Weizmann, August 5, 1934, read before the Political Committee of Mapai, *MAP* (Political Committee), August 5, 1934; *ZBG*, vol. II, p. 149.
5. Ibid.
6. Meeting of the Jewish Agency Directorate, *JAG*, May 19, 1926; *ZBG*, vol. II, p. 196.
7. Ahmad Samah al-Khalidi's proposal, on Government College Stationery, dated January 7, 1934, *CAHJP* P3/2436.
8. Undated letter from DBG to Magnes, *CAHJP* P3/2436.
9. Gabriel Cohen, "Re'ayon Haluqat Eretz-Israel ve-medina Yehudit 1933–1935," *Zionut*, vol. III.
10. For the first talk with Alami, of March 20, 1934, see *YBG*, March 20 and September 4, 1934; *PMA*, pp. 20f.; *ZBG*, vol. II, pp. 163f.
11. *MAP* (Political Committee), June 21, 1936.
12. Geoffrey Furlonge, *Palestine Is My Country: The Story of Musa Alami*. New York, Praeger, 1969, p. 103.
13. *MAP* (Political Committee), July 28, 1934; *YBG*, September 4, 1934.
14. For the talk with al-Sulh, see *PMA*, pp. 21–22; *ZBG*, vol. II, p. 164.
15. For the talk with Abd al-Hadi, see *PMA*, pp. 22–23; *ZBG*, vol. II, p. 165.
16. *YBG*, September 4, 1934; *ZBG*, vol. II, pp. 168 f.; *PMA*, pp. 29f.
17. *MAP* (Central Committee), August 8, 1934; *MAP* (Council), August 28, 1934, for Katznelson's views.
18. DBG's letter to Magnes, September 7, 1934; *ZBG*, vol. II, p. 173; *PMA*, p. 37.
19. *ZBG*, vol. II, pp. 163f.; *PMA*, pp. 25f.
20. Ibid.
21. *La Nation arabe* (Geneva), no. 2, November–December 1934, Hebrew translation in *IDF* 2847; published in *PMA*, p. 41.

22. Letter from Arslan to Akram Zuaytir concerning meeting with DBG, December 4, 1934, in *Zuaytir Papers*, Beirut, Institute for Palestine Studies.
23. Ibid.
24. *PMA*, pp. 37–39.
25. Ibid.
26. *YBG*, September 23, 1934.
27. Draft of *PMA*, in DBG's archive.
28. *Davar*, October 18, 1934; see also *Davar*, October 3 and 13, 1934.
29. Text in *ZBG*, vol. II, p. 181.
30. *YBG*, October 15, 16, 1934.
31. Ibid.
32. *Jewish Chronicle*, October 26, 1934.
33. *PMA*, pp. 43–44.
34. Ibid.
35. Draft of *PMA*, in DBG's archive.
36. DBG's letter from London to Jewish Agency, June 9, 1936, *ZBG*, vol. II, p. 254.
37. *YBG*, January 17, 1966.
38. Letter from Sharett to DBG, June 14, 1936; *ZBG*, vol. II, p. 258.

Notes to Chapter 11

1. *PMA*, p. 44.
2. "Change of Direction" in *PMA*, p. 70; DBG's letter to Lord Melchett, November 2, 1935, *ZBG*, vol. II, p. 500.
3. Conversation between Wauchope and Sharett, *PMA*, p. 68; Political Committee of Mapai, January 26, 1936, *MAP*.
4. DBG in the Political Committee of Mapai, December 2, 1935, *MAP*.
5. Sharett before Jewish Agency, February 17, 1935, *JAG*.
6. Letter from DBG to Geula and Amos, his children, September 7, 1935, *MP*, p. 105; *ZBG*, vol. II, p. 414.
7. DBG's letter to P. Rutenberg, October 14, 1935, *ZBG*, vol. II, p. 464.
8. Sharett before Mapai Political Committee, October 27, 1935, *MAP*.
9. *YBG*, December 31, 1935.
10. Eliahu Golomb in Mapai Central Committee, April 16, 1936, *MAP*.
11. Mapai Political Committee, March 9, 1936, *MAP*.
12. Ibid.
13. Ibid., April 7, 1936.
14. Ibid.
15. Ibid., March 30, 1936.

16. Ibid.
17. Mapai Central Committee, April 16, 1936, *MAP*.
18. Mapai Political Committee, January 26, 1936, *MAP*.
19. Mapai Central Committee, April 16, 1935, *MAP*.
20. Mapai Political Committee, April 7, 1936, *MAP*.
21. *YBG*, November 20, 1934.
22. Ibid.
23. *YBG*, November 24, 1924.
24. *YBG*, July 19, 1936; Sharett in the Mapai Political Committee, July 22, 1936, *MAP*.
25. *YBG*, November 24, 1935; *ZBG*, vol. II, p. 526.
26. *YBG*, March 11, 1936; Political Committee, March 30, 1936, *MAP*.
27. *AS*, p. 150.
28. DBG's letter to Nahum Goldmann, April 26, 1936; see also Sharett's letter to DBG, August 2, 1936, in *ZBG*, vol. III, p. 356.
29. Cable from Sharett to DBG, June 26, 1935, *MBG*.
30. *PMA*, p. 47.
31. The three conversations with Antonius—April 17, 22, and 29, 1936—in *MBG; PMA*, pp. 47–67; *ZBG*, vol. III, p. 130; report by DBG to Jewish Agency, June 24, 1936, *JAG*.
32. *PMA*, p. 67.
33. *YBG*, May 5, 1936; *ZBG*, vol. III, p. 176.
34. *PMA*, p. 52.
35. Ibid., pp. 48, 49.

Notes to Chapter 12

1. DBG's letter from London to Jewish Agency, June 9, 1936; *ZBG*, vol. III, p. 255.
2. *JAG*, May 19, 1936; *ZBG*, vol. III, p. 197.
3. *MAP*, September 29, 1936.
4. *JAG*, May 19, 1936.
5. See note 1 above.
6. Letter from DBG to Ussishkin, November 11, 1936; *YBG*, November 11, 1936; cf. *JAG*, October 4, 1936.
7. DBG to Va'ad Le'umi, May 5, 1936, *ZBG*, vol. III, p. 161.
8. Ibid.
9. Ibid.
10. *HISC*, February 8, 1937; *Pinkas*, no. 4, March–April 1937.
11. *MAP* (Political Committee), May 4, 1936.
12. DBG's letter to Sharett, June 24, 1937; *ZBG*, vol. IV, p. 240.

13. *MAP* (Council), January 23, 1937.
14. DBG's letter to Jewish Agency, June 9, 1936; *ZBG*, vol. III, p. 255.
15. On the debate, see DBG to Mapai Central Committee, August 11, 1936; *ZBG*, vol. III, pp. 363–368; DBG's letter to Sharett, June 18, 1936, *ZBG*, vol. III, pp. 370–373; *BK*, vol. IX, pp. 178–209; *DV*, vol. II, pp. 283–287.
16. *BK*, vol. IX, pp. 178–209.
17. Letter from DBG to Mapai Central Committee, June 18, 1936; *ZBG*, vol. III, p. 281.
18. *Ha'aretz*, February 10, 1937.
19. *HISC*, February 8, 1937.
20. *JAG*, May 19, 1936.
21. Ibid.
22. Letter from DBG to Mapai Central Committee, June 18, 1936; *ZBG*, vol. III, p. 278.
23. Letter from DBG to Sharett, June 24, 1937; *ZBG*, vol. IV, p. 278.
24. *HISC*, February 8, 1937; *Pinkas*, no. 4, March–April 1937.
25. *MAP* (Council), January 23, 1937.
26. Letter from DBG to Ussishkin (see note 6 above).
27. *MAP* (Council), January 23, 1937.
28. *YBG*, April 20, 1936.
29. Assembly of Zionist parties in Jerusalem, April 19, 1936; *ZBG*, vol. III, p. 122.
30. *AS*, pp. 160–64.
31. DBG to Va'ad Le'umi in Tel Aviv, May 5, 1936; *ZBG*, vol. III, p. 164.
32. See note 29.
33. *JAG*, May 15, 1936.
34. See note 31.
35. DBG in gathering of party colleagues, September 1939, *IDF* 2957.
36. *MAP* (Central Committee), July 6, 1938; DBG's speech to Twenty-first Zionist Congress, August 21, 1939, *IDF* 2957.
37. *YBG*, July 11, 1936.
38. Letter from DBG to Mapai Central Committee, August 11, 1936; *ZBG*, vol. III, p. 365.
39. Ibid.
40. *MAP* (Central Committee), July 6, 1938.

Notes to *Chapter* 13

1. *YBG*, February 22, 1938; *MAP* (Central Committee), April 4, 1938.
2. DBG in speech in Tel Aviv, September 10, 1936; *ZBG*, vol. III, p. 411.
3. Ibid.
4. *JAG*, May 15, 1936.
5. *MAP* (Central Committee), June 9, 1936.
6. Norman Rose, *The Gentile Zionists*. London, Frank Cass, 1973, pp. 127–128.
7. *MAP* (Political Consultation), June 8, 1937.
8. Letter from DBG to Sharett, July 3, 1937; *ZBG*, vol. IV, p. 297.
9. *YBG*, July 7, 12, 1937.
10. *YBG*, July 12, 1937; *ZBG*, vol. IV, p. 298.
11. Ibid.
12. Letter from DBG to Amos, July 27, 1937; *ZBG*, vol. IV, p. 331.
13. *YBG*, July 12, 1937; *ZBG*, vol. IV, p. 299.
14. Letter to Amos (see note 12 above).
15. Report of Partition (Woodhead) Commission (Cmd. 5854); Palestine: statement by His Majesty's Government (Cmd. 5893).
16. Letter from DBG to Sharett, *YBG*, September 20, 1938.
17. Letter from DBG to Katznelson, *YBG*, March 16, 1938.
18. Letter from DBG to to his children, *YBG*, October 7, 1938.
19. Letter from DBG to Dov Joseph, *YBG*, October 18, 1938.
20. Conversation with Harold MacMichael, *YBG*, February 22, 1938.
21. *HISC*, July 25–26, 1938.
22. *ZER*, October 26, 1936.
23. *MAP* (Council), January 19, 1933.
24. *MAP* (Central Committee), April 16, 1936.
25. *YBG*, December 5, 1936.
26. *HISC*, December 5, 1936.
27. Report by DBG, September 8, 1939, *IDF* 2957; *STH*, vol. II, part 3, p. 1392.
28. DBG's closed speech at the Zionist Congress, August 5, 1937; *YBG*, October 29, 1937.
29. *YBG*, February 22, 1938.
30. DBG's letter to Dr. Moshe Sneh, July 20, 1937; *ZBG*, vol. IV, p. 310.
31. See note 27 above.
32. Letter from DBG to his children, October 7, 1938; *MP*, p. 252.
33. *YBG*, September 10, 1937; ZBG, vol. IV, p. 433.
34. Letter from DBG to Amos, October 5, 1937, *IDF* 3121, full text; a heavily edited text appears in *MP*, p. 210.

35. Ibid.
36. *YBG*, October 29, 1937.
37. *MAP* (Central Committee), April 16, 1936.
38. Ibid., April 10, 1937.
39. DBG's letter to Jewish Agency, *YBG*, October 3, 1938.
40. *YBG*, September 15, 1938.
41. DBG before Tel Aviv workers, July 27, 1939, *IDF* 2957.
42. Letter from DBG to Sharett, *YBG*, September 20, 1938.
43. *MAP* (Central Committee), December 7, 1938.
44. Letter from DBG to his children, October 7, 1938; *MP*, p. 248.
45. See note 41. For MacDonald's version see meeting of February 15, 1939, *FO* 371/23224.
46. Ibid.
47. Ibid.
48. Ibid.
49. *YBG*, January 3, 1939.
50. *YBG*, April 1, 1939.
51. See note 35 to Chapter Twelve.
52. *MAP* (Central Committee), September 12, 1939.
53. *YBG*, April 4, 1941.
54. DBG's speech to World Council of United Poalei Zion, August 4, 1937; *ZBG*, vol. IV, p. 374.

Notes to Epilogue

1. *MAP* (Council), April 14, 1939.
2. DBG's letter to Brandeis, December 6, 1940, *MBG*.
3. Ibid.
4. *JAG*, October 22, 1939.

Index